Cuddesdon and Dorchester-on-Thames, Oxfordshire:

two early Saxon 'princely' sites in Wessex

Tania M. Dickinson

British Archaeological Reports 1
1974

BRITISH ARCHAEOLOGICAL REPORTS

122, Banbury Road, Oxford OX2 7BP, England

General Editors:

    A.R.Hands, B.Sc., M.A., D.Phil.

    Mrs Y.M.Hands

    D.R.Walker, B.A.

Advisory Editors:

    C.B.Burgess, M.A.

    Neil Cossons, M.A., F.S.A., F.M.A.

    Professor B.W.Cunliffe, M.A., Ph.D., F.S.A.

    Sonia Chadwick Hawkes, B.A., M.A., F.S.A.

    Professor G.D.B.Jones, M.A., D.Phil., F.S.A.

    Frances Lynch, M.A., F.S.A.

    P.A.Mellars, M.A., Ph.D.

    P.A.Rahtz, M.A., F.S.A.

B.A.R. 1, 1974: "Cuddesdon and Dorchester-on-Thames"

© Tania M. Dickinson, 1974

ISBN 9780904531008 paperback
ISBN 9781407318219 e-book
DOI https://doi.org/10.30861/9780904531008
A catalogue record for this book is available from the British Library
This book is available at www.barpublishing.com

CUDDESDON AND DORCHESTER-ON-THAMES

CONTENTS

LIST OF PLATES

LIST OF TEXT FIGURES

ACKNOWLEDGEMENTS

My greatest debt is to Professor and Mrs. C. F. C. Hawkes, who have, at all times, encouraged, criticised and assisted me; Mrs. Hawkes has given me information on Kentish material, especially from her unpublished excavation at Finglesham, and allowed me to quote this. Dr. J. N. L. Myres and Mr. J. Campbell kindly read an earlier draft of this paper, and offered much constructive criticism. The following have generously given assistance on specific topics: Miss U. Slevogt on the Cuddesdon glass bowls, Mr. S. E. Rigold and Dr. J. P. C. Kent on the Dorchester gold coins, and Mr. J. McN. Dodgson on the place-names. Mr. J. H. Kelly of Stoke-on-Trent Museum identified for me the nineteenth-century china from Cuddesdon.

I am indebted to the Church Commission and the former Lord Bishop of Oxford, the Rt. Rev. Harry Carpenter, for permission to excavate at Cuddesdon, to the Meyerstein Fund of Oxford University which financed the work, and to all those who participated. I am most grateful to Mrs. Boughton-Leigh for permission to publish her glass bowl from Cuddesdon, to the Society of Antiquaries of London for permission to publish Plate IVb, and to the Ashmolean Museum, Oxford, for Plates IIa and b.

I am also grateful to Miss Anna Kilner and Mrs. Brigid Campbell for undertaking the examination of the bones from Cuddesdon, to Mr. R. L. Wilkins who prepared the photographs, to Mrs. M. Cox who drew Figure 3, and to Mrs. E. A. Lowe who typed these pages. Finally, my husband, Dr. Oliver Dickinson, has been a continual help in the production of this monograph.

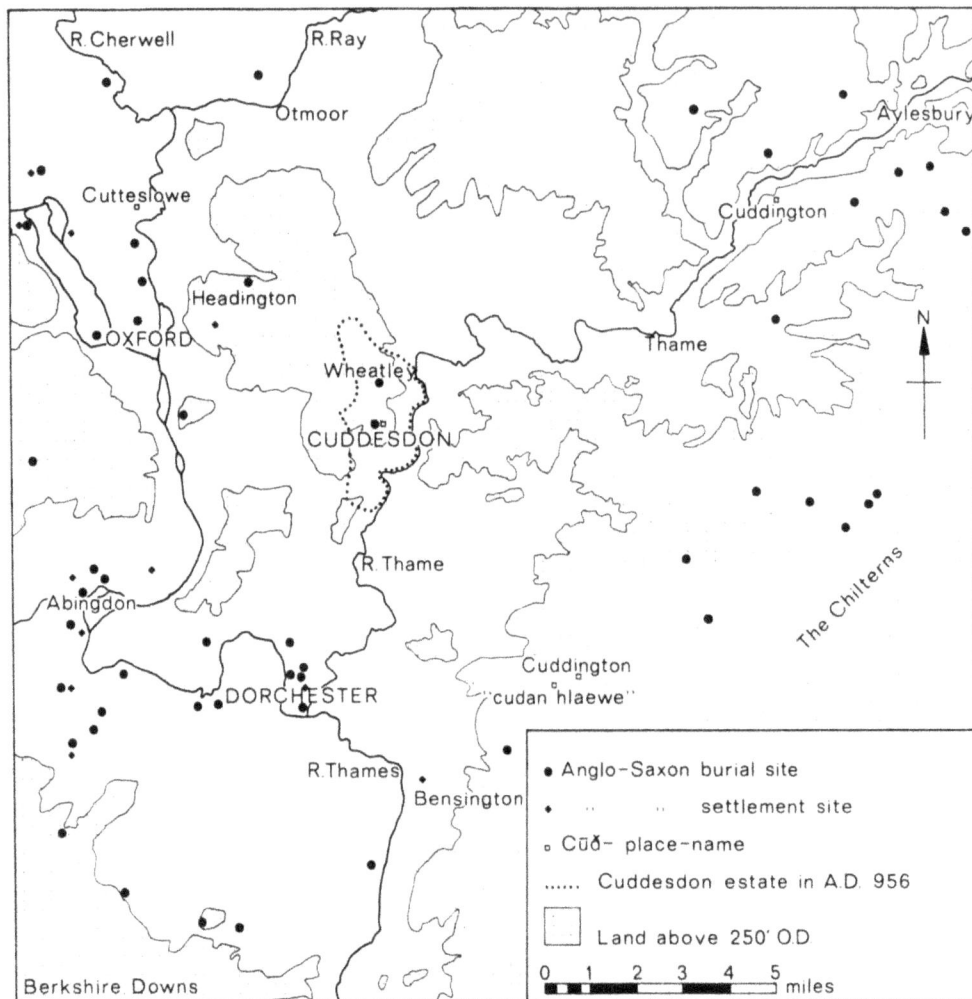

FIG. 1 – Map of the area around Cuddesdon and Dorchester-on-Thames showing the distribution of Cūð- prototheme place-names and of Anglo-Saxon burial and settlement sites of the period A. D. 400–700.

INTRODUCTION

The Sutton Hoo ship-burial is the foremost of a remarkable group of graves of the late sixth and early seventh centuries A. D. These are, besides the great ship-burial, the other three excavated mounds at Sutton Hoo[1], and the graves at Taplow (Bucks)[2], Broomfield (Essex)[3] and Coombe (Kent)[4]. All burials of males, and all except Broomfield under barrow-mounds, they include the richest Anglo-Saxon graves known, and they exhibit a close inter-relationship in burial rites, individual grave-goods, and grave-assemblages as a whole.

The intensive study of the Sutton Hoo ship-burial has naturally cast light on the others; in particular, it provides a yardstick for their dating[5] and for estimations of their social status. It far excels the rest in grave-furniture, but then it is clearly the burial of an East Anglian king, if not of Raedwald the Bretwalda. The others can hardly be of much lower status, particularly since Sutton Hoo seems likely to have been the royal cemetery of East Anglia at this period[6]; they could be termed "princely" [7].

The graves listed are the best and most certain examples of this class; further examples may be discovered, since only Sutton Hoo can be related to one of the major royal families of the period, and one might expect to find such graves in the other kingdoms[8]. I wish to discuss existing evidence for one, possibly two, in the Upper Thames valley, an important area of the kingdom of Wessex.

The evidence consists of chance finds made in the eighteenth century at Dorchester-on-Thames and in 1847 at Cuddesdon. These were recorded and published in a summary fashion, and most of the objects have since been lost. Despite the obvious limitations such material presents to re-interpretation, I hope by a detailed examination to demonstrate a clear relationship with the "princely" burials. I shall begin with Cuddesdon, for which there is more documentation, and bring the history of finds there

1

up-to-date with an account of my own excavations before dealing with the more glamorous nineteenth-century discoveries; I shall then examine the relevant material from Dorchester-on-Thames, and conclude with some comments on the historical significance of this material.

I. CUDDESDON

HISTORY OF THE FINDS (Figs. 1 and 2)

The village of Cuddesdon lies on the southern flank of a spur of high ground, which projects towards the River Thame from the outcrop of oolitic limestone to the east of Oxford. The summit of the hill is capped by a thick deposit of sand (National Grid reference SP 600031; 350' O.D.). In the seventeenth century this commanding site was chosen for the Bishop of Oxford's episcopal palace[9]. The Anglo-Saxon discoveries were made when in 1847 Bishop Samuel Wilberforce decided to enlarge this palace and empark his estate.

The only record of the events is an anonymous communication to the Archaeological Journal for that year (vol. IV, 157-9). It is both ambiguous and inadequate; any interpretation depends to a considerable degree on certain key phrases (my underlining):-

"In the course of some alterations made by the Bishop of Oxford in the beginning of the present year, in front of the gateway of the episcopal palace at Cuddesden (sic), the workmen, while digging for making a new carriage-way, discovered several human skeletons at the depth of between two and three feet from the surface. On further examination it was found that the skeletons were arranged in a circle, their heads outwards, lying on their faces with their legs crossed. They were in a high state of preservation. Near them were found several highly curious and interesting objects, ..."

These were two swords, two squat blue glass bowls, a bronze bucket, a fragment of gilt bronze set with garnets, and a late medieval ring. They all passed into the care of the Bishop, who exhibited them to the Society of Antiquaries of London on 9 November, 1852, but the notice of this adds no new information[10]. Three years later J. Y. Akerman republished the glass vessels and the bucket[11], and until recently he was the last person known to have seen the Cuddesdon finds. Copies of Akerman's engravings have

3

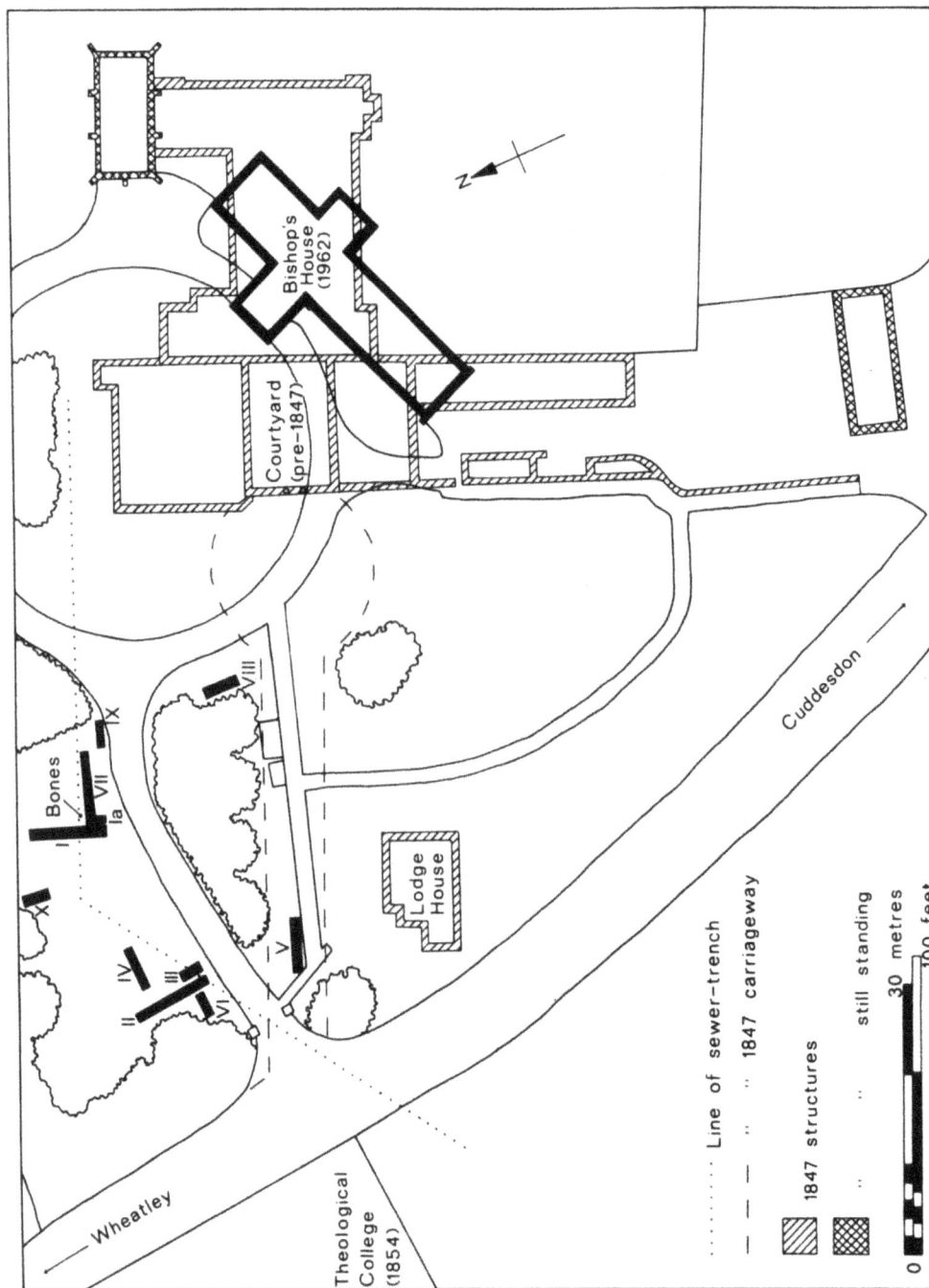

FIG. 2 – Plan of the grounds of The Bishop's House, Cuddesdon, showing the buildings of the former episcopal palace and the 1970 excavation trenches.

appeared in several works, and the glass vessels and the bucket are commonly cited in studies dealing with their respective class of object[12].

E. T. Leeds initially believed that the glass vessels were in the British Museum[13], no doubt confusing them with the similar pair from Broomfield; later he realised his mistake and attempted, unsuccessfully, to trace the whereabouts of the material[14]. In 1971 a series of most fortunate coincidences led to the rediscovery of one of the glass bowls in the private possession of Mrs. Boughton-Leigh, of Newbold-upon-Avon, near Rugby. Unfortunately, it is not known how the bowl came into the family's possession, so that no clues have been provided as to the whereabouts of the other objects, which remain, at the moment, lost.

The exact site of the finds is uncertain. They were made "in front of the gateway" and on the line of "the new carriageway". This has generally been assumed to mean the spot where the driveway joined the Wheatley-Cuddesdon road, opposite the Theological College[15], but there is another possibility. It will be necessary to discuss Bishop Wilberforce's alterations in some detail to explain this (see Fig. 2).

Before 1847 the episcopal palace was an H-shaped building with its front door in the centre of the long north side. On the short west side there was a courtyard, abutting on to the old Wheatley-Cuddesdon lane, which the front driveway must also have joined in a sweeping curve. Although the courtyard led immediately to the serving quarters, it had a very fine gateway[16]. Wilberforce turned this courtyard into his front entrance and the gateway into a front door; from them he built a carriage-way to the new Wheatley-Cuddesdon road, which had been moved westwards to allow for the emparking of the estate[17], and new gates at the road junction[18].

After these alterations, the new gateway would naturally be assumed to be the one meant by the original report, and Akerman's substitution of the word "road" for the carriage-way of the original report may have strengthened this belief[19].

However, in 1847 an unqualified reference to "the gateway" would surely be taken to mean the gates eventually converted to a front door, which were far more impressive than the new ones. Moreover, it is not at all clear when, in relation to the discoveries, the new gates were built! It is thus perfectly possible that the old gates were meant, and the results of the 1970 excavation seem to support this view.

EXCAVATIONS AT THE BISHOP'S HOUSE, CUDDESDON, 1970 (Fig. 2).

In 1970 I carried out a trial excavation to discover whether any new information could be gained about the 1847 finds. The chance of discovering undisturbed Saxon material was slight from the outset: the entire area had been extensively disturbed by the demolition in 1962 of the old palace, unoccupied since 1937, the erection of a new house, the digging of a driveway to the north of the former one, and the landscaping of the garden. The area closest to the more likely site of the original finds was covered by tarmac or lawn and could not be disturbed. The ground available for exploration was, therefore, very restricted, and the situation was made worse by the fact that an 11 ft. deep sewer-trench, probably contemporary with the 1847 works, ran across this site. Since circumstances did not permit a large or mechanised labour force, excavation was carried out in ten trial-trenches, each one metre wide.

Trench I was originally aligned to determine the width of disturbance caused by the sewer-trench. In fact, the edges of the sewer-trench could not be defined within the length of Trench I. Below the top-soil the section showed a central V-shaped core of hard yellow sand, the southern side lying partly over a tipped layer of dark brown soil full of cinders and household china dating from c. 1850 - c. 1914. Although the V-shaped core appeared as a later filling-up of the sewer, it may have been the path through the shrubbery shown in maps of the estate along the line of the sewer[20].

Below these two layers there was light brown sand merging imperceptibly into bright yellow sand; the former appeared to have been cut through by the V-shaped core. Since finds were made in both the light brown and bright yellow layers, it is presumed that they were the original fill of the sewer-trench. As the purpose of the investigation was not an excavation of a nineteenth-century sewer-trench the stratigraphy was taken no deeper.

Trench VII was dug at a right-angle to Trench I along the length of the sewer-trench. At their junction, in the two lower sand layers, a quantity of disarticulated human bone was found, with small bones, such as metacarpals, scattered sporadically along the length of Trench VII. A tile was found with the main concentration of bones. Apart from Trench V, which cut through part of the old carriage-way, all the other trenches revealed only root and animal disturbance of the sub-soil.

The human bones represented a minimum number of four bodies: a child aged between eight and puberty, one female about twenty years old, another adult female and an adult male (see Appendix I, below p. 37). They were in an excellent state of preservation and there seems no reason to doubt that they are some of the skeletons originally found in 1847. The concentration of large bones at one point and thin scatter of small bones elsewhere suggests the deliberate gathering together and disposal of the skeletal material in the nearest open hole, in this case the upper filling of the sewer-trench. The site of the original discovery is likely to have been close at hand.

There were only two other finds which deserve mention. The first is a lace-tag found at the eastern end of Trench VII in the same layer which produced the scatter of small bones. It is made of sheet bronze rolled into a cylinder 2.55cm long, which tapered to a closed end; the other, broader end was open and a minute bronze rivet passed through it. It enclosed a fragment of cloth or threads (Fig. 3a).

The date of this lace-tag remains uncertain. Tubular shoe-lace tags, which seem to fall into two types, are known from a number of seventh-century Anglo-Saxon cemeteries. The first type has been listed and discussed by Mrs. S. C. Hawkes in relation to the finds at Winnall (Hants) and Shakenoak (Oxon)[21]. They are all about 2.0 - 3.0cm long, cylindrical, and split at the upper end to form two flat tabs, which are fastened by a rivet. The examples from Burwell (Camb) and Horndean (Sussex) show a moulding to the body and a spatulate tip, not found on those from Stanton Harcourt (Oxon) and Winnall. The second type is a hollow cone of rolled sheet bronze, also about 2.0 - 3.0cm long, and not necessarily riveted. There are three from Finglesham (Kent), graves 68, 163 and 180, the first and last being richly-equipped burials probably dating to the middle

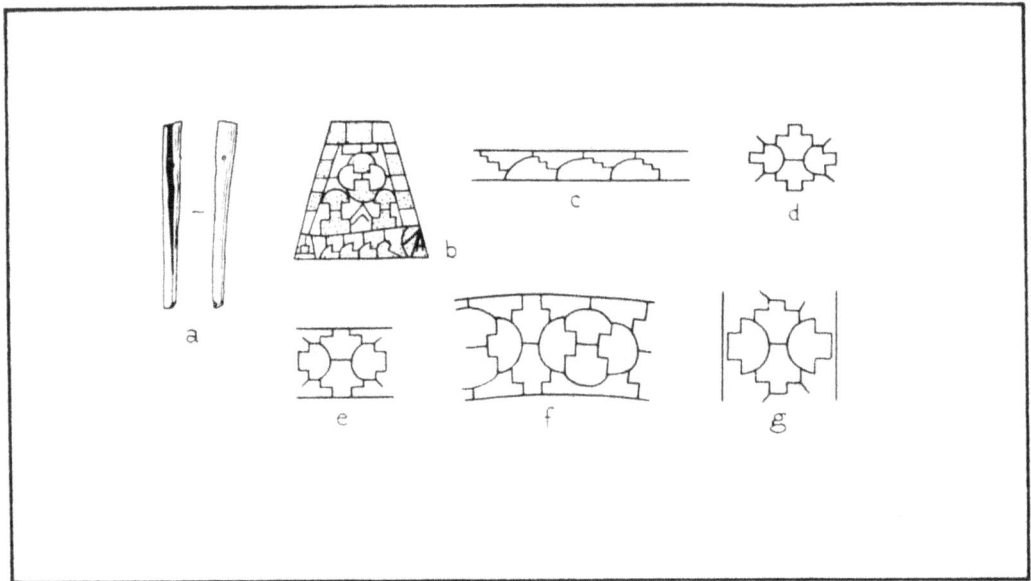

FIG. 3 - (a) Cuddesdon lace-tag, Sc. 1/1; (b) Dorchester pyramidal stud, Sc. 1/1; (c) - (g) garnet cell-work elements, not to scale: (c) and (d) Sutton Hoo (after Bruce-Mitford 1972); (e) Tongres ornament (after Bruce-Mitford 1949); (f) Egbert shrine disc, Trier; (g) Wilton Cross (after Bruce-Mitford 1949).

or later seventh century. Similar bronze cones are recorded from Kingston Down (Kent), graves 185 and 211[22]. Those tags which have closely datable associations, the two from Finglesham and Burwell grave 83, suggest a date in the middle or late seventh century; but an earlier date is not precluded since they occur in poorly-furnished graves, which are undatable.

In fact, the closest Saxon parallel to the Cuddesdon tag, which does not conform exactly to either of the above groups, is also the earliest tag of which I know. It is a simple rolled sheet of bronze without a rivet (length 3.4cm) from grave 123 at Sleaford (Lincs)[23], now in the National Museum of Wales. Originally, there were two, associated with a pair of simple sheet bronze sleeve-clasps, as if they came from wrist, not shoe or leg, fastenings. The grave contained a cruciform brooch of Åberg's later Group III, which may imply a date about 500 A.D., or a little after[24].

It is possible, however, that the Cuddesdon tag is not of Saxon date. At least eighty fragments of precisely similar sheet bronze tags, some with rivets, others without, were found in 1965 in a well-stratified fifteenth-century level in the abbey church at Cirencester[25], so that it could be medieval.

The other find is only mentioned because it might interest those concerned with problems of coin-dating. It was a royal farthing of Charles I, a Maltravers "round" (1634-36)[26], which was a chance find from the sub-humus layer of Trench VI. Its date coincides exactly with the building of the first episcopal palace.

The recovery of some of the original skeletal material was thus the only positive contribution made by the 1970 excavation. Considering that the extensive disturbances of the site by building and landscaping, as well as the excavation trenches, have produced no record of further finds, it now seems unlikely that there ever was any extensive cemetery adjacent to the original group of burials found in 1847. The chance of recovering any further information about the nineteenth-century discoveries is now very remote.

THE 1847 FINDS

The mainly negative results produced by the excavation, taken with the
fact that only one of the lost objects has been located, force any further
enquiry to return to the records of the original discoveries, which, as I
have emphasised, are ambiguous and inadequate. The meaning of certain
phrases becomes of prime importance, if good sense is to be made of the
report as a whole. The discussion of the objects necessitates one crucial
decision at the outset.

The 1847 report states that the objects were discovered "near" the
circle of inhumations. Taken literally, this implies that the skeletons
themselves had no grave-goods and that the objects were found as a single
assemblage a little distant from the burials. Since such deposits are not
known from Anglo-Saxon England except in funerary contexts, they could
then represent part or all of a single grave-group, and their parallels with
the group of "princely" burials mentioned make this a very attractive
theory. But in view of the circumstances and poor recording of the find,
this might seem a rash conclusion and certain arguments can be advanced
for the view that "near" is simply loose nineteenth-century usage for "with",
and that the objects are grave-goods of some of the skeletons in the circle:

1. The skeletons found in the 1970 excavation form a varied group that
   could be part of a normal family or community cemetery, whose
   burials might be expected to have had grave-goods.

2. Swords normally occur singly (even the Sutton Hoo ship-burial had only
   one) and the occurrence of two should represent two furnished male
   burials.

3. The number of recorded items is low, and there is a notable lack of
   personal jewellery; there is a possibility that some were overlooked
   or concealed, so that the recorded ones might be a very unrepresent-
   ative sample, upon which it would be unwise to base conclusions[27].
   These arguments have force, but they are open to criticism:

1. Two distinctive features separate Cuddesdon from normal cemeteries,
   the radial lay-out of the skeletons and the fact that all were lying face
   downward. Radial burials are rare, but there are two definite cases

of such an arrangement where the bodies were accompanied by normal Anglo-Saxon grave-goods. Uniform prone burial is unique, and combined with a radial lay-out, it makes the Cuddesdon cemetery very unusual indeed (see below, p. 19).

2. There are examples of two swords with a single burial, most notably at Coombe[28], where the swords were wrapped in cloth and placed unburnt in the grave. The second sword, regrettably, did not survive the initial recording of the grave, but I see no reason to doubt its existence: it would seem that there was only one male cremated, since there was only one spear, and probably one axe[29]. Abroad, male burials with two swords are known from several graves in Sweden, from graves 6 and 7 at Valsgärde[30], and from graves I and XII at Vendel[31], all of which probably date to the end of the sixth century and the seventh century.

The custom of burying a sword and seax together is found in richer continental graves from the fifth century onwards[32], though it is very rare in England: graves 10 and 56 at Gilton (Kent), both datable to about the middle of the sixth century, had narrow seaxes[33], a larger seax was laid just to the south of the sword in the Sutton Hoo ship-burial[34], and a somewhat short, broad seax came from grave 58 at Sibertswold (Kent), presumably of seventh-century date[35]. Since the Cuddesdon swords were said to have been in a poor, and probably unrecognisable, condition, a seax may have been mistaken for a sword. Faussett frequently described seaxes which he excavated in Kent during the eighteenth century as a "short sword or dagger", and though a short narrow seax is quite different from a long sword, one cannot expect nineteenth-century workmen to use distinguishing terminology. If there were two swords at Coombe, then two swords at Cuddesdon is less unthinkable; if there were a sword and a seax at Cuddesdon, and it is always possible that this was the case at Coombe, then again there is no need to envisage two graves.

3. If the number of recorded objects is small for a single burial, it would be minute for several, particularly since one would expect graves

equipped with the fine recorded pieces to have held many others of similar quality. It does not seem possible that so much could have gone
unrecorded. Small objects from a single grave may well have been
overlooked: if the grave had been robbed in antiquity, as is only too
possible, the resulting disorder and disarticulation, or even removal,
of the corpse, might explain why the nineteenth-century workmen were
so vague about the nature of their discovery.

The arguments against treating these goods as a single group can thus
be countered. The most compelling argument for such a view will appear
from the discussion of the finds, which brings one back again and again
to the same group of "princely" burials; these parallels make it far more
likely that the Cuddesdon finds are the remains from a single rich grave
rather than the gleanings of several.

(a) The glass bowls (**Pls. I and II**)

The glass bowls were first drawn and described in the Archaeological
Journal, and then, independently, examined and published by Akerman.
Until the rediscovery of one of the bowls, there had been considerable
uncertainty as to the interpretation of these two slightly differing accounts.
Both bowls were described as "of a very pale blue transparent glass, the
surface of which has become iridescent from decomposition"; yet Akerman's illustration of them is coloured a dense, dark grey-blue. In fact, as
can now be seen, bowl 2 is made from a dark royal blue metal, translucent
when held to the light, but opaque against a dark background, and it is covered with a fine iridescent bloom. It contains few bubbles, but inclusions
in the glass have produced a diagonally streaked effect. This type of glass
is typical of the vessels quoted as parallels below, and assuming that both
bowls were similar, the description of the glass of bowl 2 would also apply
to bowl 1.

Less important is the slight discrepancy between recorded measurements and the drawn proportions of bowl 1. It was said to be the larger,
measuring 3" in height and $5^7/8$" in diameter, but both the engravings give
a height of $3\frac{1}{4}$"(8.5cm) and a diameter of $4\frac{1}{2}$" (11.5cm). It is a squat bowl
with an upright "collar" neck and sharp shoulder, below which are three

thick, applied glass trails. They were laid on straight, or with a slight wave, and then pinched out, alternately upwards and downwards, to form two rows of lozenge-shaped cells. The base is marked by a pattern around its circumference, again formed by the application of a thick trail, which was pulled towards the centre at intervals, producing what the Archaeological Journal called "cusping".

In Dr. D. B. Harden's classification of Anglo-Saxon glass, bowl 1 belongs to his group VIIIa iv[36], which is distinctive for its dark blue glass, as well as its form. In 1964 Dr. Bruce-Mitford brought the list of examples up-to-date[37]. A fragment of blue glass from the Snape (Suffolk) boat-grave, which he assigns to this class, would be the earliest recorded example, datable to the mid-sixth century[38]; but it is far from certain that the fragment was really from a class VIIIa iv bowl, since neither its shape nor shade of blue is known[39]. Bruce-Mitford also lists two Norwegian and three English sites, apart from Cuddesdon, to which may be added a bowl recently acquired by the British Museum. Both Norwegian examples probably came from barrow-burials. The one from Tu i Klepp, which certainly did, is dated by the associated brooches to the later sixth century, but the associations of the other bowl are unknown.

Of the English bowls, two come from Kentish cemeteries, one definitely a rich cemetery, and two from burials of my "princely" group. The pair of bowls from Broomfield[40] were found together with beech-wood cups and part of a drinking horn in a sheet-bronze bowl, a deposit similar to that of burr-wood cups found inside a small silver dish and below the "Anastasius" dish in the Sutton Hoo ship-burial[41]. The Broomfield grave also contained a garnet and glass cloisonné "shield", originally from a buckle, probably one with a triangular plate, and possibly decorated with zoomorphic filigree work, datable to about 600 A. D. or later[42]. The gold and garnet pyramidal stud from the grave supports this early seventh-century date (see below, p. 27 for a discussion of pyramidal studs).

Sutton Hoo mound 2, the second ship-burial, contained fragments of a blue glass vessel of Cuddesdon type[43]. The burial must be very close in date to the major ship-burial since they share the same die-stamp on the triangular vandykes from their drinking horns, and there are strong stylistic similarities between the mound 2 zoomorphic interlace disc, very similar to the disc from the Caenby (Lincs) barrow-burial[44], and the Sutton Hoo mound 1 great gold buckle, which suggest that they belong to the same chronological horizon, that is the third decade of the seventh century.

A pair of bowls was discovered at Aylesford (Kent)[45], but the burials, found in 1922, were not carefully recorded and the individual objects which were kept cannot be related to graves. This is particularly unfortunate, as the large composite disc-brooch, belonging to Leed's Class III and possibly among its later versions[46], and the Frankish pottery jugs suggest that some of the graves belonged to the first third of the seventh century. As it is, neither the status nor the chronological context of the burial, to which the bowls belonged, are assured. The British Museum has recently acquired another bowl, which was discovered by accident at The Beeches, St. Richard's Road, Deal (Kent), but the rest of the grave, from which it must have come, has not been investigated.

The glass of bowl 2 has been described above. There was originally a thicker iridescent layer on the base, but it seems to have been chipped off in modern times. There is one small patch, of about 6.0cm diameter, over the upper part of the bowl, which is completely free of decomposition, possibly because this portion of the bowl was protected by some other item in the grave. Both the flat-topped rim and base are worn. The bowl has a short upright neck, a smooth round body and an indented, badly cracked base. A thin, applied glass trail forms ten horizontal lines round the upper half; round the lower half are thirteen vertical loops, which reach right to the base. It is 9.1cm high, with a maximum diameter of 11.5cm and a rim diameter of 6.2cm. Harden placed this bowl in his class VIIIa iii. There are certainly resemblances, but all the other members of that group show widely-spaced, often lop-sided, horizontal trails, and a similar treatment of the vertical loops, which are sometimes nearer to semi-circles[47]. They bear a close resemblance in the decorative treatment to the class VIIa pouch-bottles with neck spiral and body zig-zag in a continuous trail. The Cuddesdon vessel with its neat horizontal trails and its close-set vertical loops is unique amongst known squat bowls.

Dark blue glass seems to have been a particularly seventh-century feature. Harden quotes twenty-two examples of all classes[48], over half of which are said to have come from Faversham (Kent), as, indeed, does half of the total number of squat jars. Despite the rarity of vessels like the Cuddesdon ones, it is probable that they are both of English manufacture. The late sixth-century context of the bowl from Tu i Klepp implies that they were already being made before 600. The rims of the bowls from Sutton Hoo mound 2, Broomfield and Aylesford, as well as bowl 2 from Cuddesdon, all show considerable wear, which suggests that they had had a long life before burial. Since dating evidence from all the English graves favours a time of deposition in the early seventh century, it seems reasonable to place a similar date on the Cuddesdon burial.

(b) The bronze bucket (Pl. III)

Akerman examined the bucket, and his publication adds some new information. His measurements vary in some details from those given in the Archaeological Journal; and his engraving, which is at a scale of about 5 : 9, does not quite correspond to the recorded proportions. The bucket was approximately 9" (22.8cm) high, with an internal depth of $8\frac{1}{4}$" (21.0cm), outside rim diameter of $8\frac{5}{8}$" (21.9cm), inside rim diameter of $7\frac{7}{8}$" (20.0cm) and an external base diameter of 5" (12.7cm); the thickness of the metal was about $\frac{1}{16}$" (0.15cm). The engraving by Orlando Jewitt in the Archaeological Journal similarly differs in some minor details of design from James Basire's in Akerman's publication; it is clear from their other works that Basire was the more faithful draughtsman.

The bucket was in very good condition, with a thin incrustation of copper oxides with "ferruginous" patches, no doubt derived from the sand in which it had lain. The handle, the handle-sockets and the two hoops around the body were made of a heavy solid metal, but Akerman noted that the body itself was of a lighter metal, which he thought resembled sheet-bronze. There is no evidence that the hoops were attached to the body by rivets, and the entire vessel was probably cast like the others of the class to which it belongs. The lower of the two hoops was rectangular in section

15

and situated just above the narrow foot; this feature, it was suggested, allowed the bucket to be stood in a trivet. The other rib, semicircular in section, was placed halfway up the body. The handle had a thickened central moulding for the hand-grip, and terminals bent at right-angles to swivel inside hollow domed sockets, which stood upright on the flat out-turned rim. The rim had been broken in antiquity and repaired with a sheet-bronze patch, held on by rivets. Engraved horizontal lines decorated the body and lower hoop.

Sir James Conway was first to identify the bucket as Coptic[49], quoting as a parallel a bucket, no. 9051 in the Cairo Museum, said to have come from Thebes (measurements: H. 20.5cm, upper diam. 19.0cm, lower diam. 13.0)[50]. It is comparable with the Cuddesdon bucket in size and in its bossed sockets for the handle, central moulding on the handle and projecting flange about two-thirds of the way down, equivalent in function to the Cuddesdon bucket's lower hoop. Its main difference is that it stands on three little feet, as does a smaller and less elegant bucket from Tomb B 37 at Ballana[51]. A third published example, which is also small, came from Giza[52]. There is a miniature bucket (H. 6.4cm) in the Ashmolean Museum (Accession number 1956.955), regrettably unprovenanced, the handle and rim of which are identical to the Cuddesdon bucket, though the convex body is quite different.

These buckets seem to have been made in the Near East between the fourth and sixth centuries, but Coptic bronze vessels do not appear as imports in Europe until the end of the sixth century, and they are primarily a feature of the seventh[53]. As might be expected of such luxury imports, they occur only in the very richest graves. In England outside Kent, two are without reliable contexts, one is from the great cemetery of Caistor-by-Norwich (Norfolk), and four (excluding the Cuddesdon example) are from rich barrow-burials; the eleven Kentish examples are from amongst the richest graves found there to date. It is a point worth noting that, whereas the bulk of the continental and all the Kentish imports of Coptic vessels are of the more common varieties, mainly Werner's type Bi (a bowl with drop-handles and an openwork foot-stand) and Bii (a pan with a dovetail handle), in England outside Kent there is a quite disproportionate number of rarities. Two East Anglian examples and possibly the fragment from the Asthall (Oxon) barrow belong, like the Kentish ones, to the class Bi bowls. On the other hand, the bowl from Sutton Hoo mound 1 is unusual and was classed by Professor Werner as a "transitional" piece between types A and B; whilst the lid from mound 3 may have come from a vessel like the bizarre "tea-pot" from Wheathampstead (Herts), which does have three parallels in Germany. But the pedestal-bowl from Taplow has only three parallels in Egypt and none north of the Alps[54], whilst the Cuddesdon bucket is rare in Egypt and apparently unique in Europe.

I do not intend to explore this observation fully here, but it does raise the question of the conditions governing the "laws" of exchange, which allowed objects of apparently great rarity to find their way to the extreme border of the distribution area. The uniform and fairly dense distribution of one of the standard types in Kent may be interpreted as the result of more regular trade, but the isolated examples may have arrived at their final destination by some other process. It casts an interesting light on the standing of some of the English ruling families that they were able to acquire such unique, and presumably prestigious, objects, perhaps as gifts.

(c) The bronze fragment (Pl. IVa)

At the time of discovery this object was already in a fragmentary condition, and neither the description nor the engraving reveal exactly from what it might have come. The bronze was originally gilded. There appears to have been an upper plaque, to one end of which three bronze strips had been fastened by rivets, their heads set probably with cabochon garnets (the 1847 report suggested carbuncles or rubies), and surrounded by beaded collars. Another, larger flat-topped garnet was set on the upper plaque, and may have been merely decorative. Two of the bronze strips were decorated with longitudinal ribbing, but the outer, right-hand one had a simple two-strand interlace below the garnet-headed rivet, and diagonal ribbing above it. It is not clear what this diagonal ribbing, which also occurred on the edge of the plaque, and part of some fan-shaped ribbing apparently below the plaque, were meant to signify: they might have been corrosion, or other decorated strips. The other end of the plaque has curved edges.

Mr. George Speake has pointed out to me that the plaque could be reconstructed as an eagle's head, with the large garnet representing its eye, and that it would then closely resemble the ornamental plaques from the Sutton Hoo ship-burial musical instrument. Certainly, the profile of the bird-head, the ribbed side-strip and the position of the large garnet stud can all be paralleled on these mounts, and to a lesser extent on the similar mounts from Taplow[55], though not the three strips held by garnet studs. Similar bird-heads occur on other mounts and inlays in the Sutton Hoo ship-burial, for example the gilt bronze extensions of the shield-grip[56], so that the Cuddesdon fragment need not imply the existence of a musical instrument in the grave.

Another object reminiscent of the Cuddesdon fragment is worth bringing into the discussion. It is the chape on the seax-scabbard from the Ford (Wilts) barrow-burial[57] which was composed of a small bronze bird's head. The slightly wider strip with interlace on the Cuddesdon fragment could be interpreted as the rigid outer edging of a scabbard, the ribbed strips as appliqués either fastening longitudinally on the front of the scabbard, or, hinged by their rivets, lying at a diagonal and linking to one or both of the scabbard edges, like the similar ribbed strip on the Ford chape. If the Cuddesdon fragment were a chape, it would still be difficult to know whether it came from a sword or seax, since there is no indication of the scale of the engraving, though it does seem larger than the Ford chape. The possibility that there was both a sword and seax in the Cuddesdon grave leaves the choice open.

But since there is no evidence that the edges of the Cuddesdon fragment were U-sectioned, a normally essential feature of chapes, and since the Ford burial should be dated to the later, rather than the earlier, seventh century, it may be preferable to regard the Cuddesdon fragment as the remains of an ornamental mount from some unknown object.

(d) The swords

There is little to add to the remarks already made about the weapons at Cuddesdon. If there were two swords in the grave, then it would indeed be an outstanding burial, both in comparison with the general sparsity of sword-graves in the Upper Thames region, and with the weapon-assemblages of rich graves in the rest of the country. If the more reasonable explanation that there was a sword and a seax is accepted, then the burial is still something of a rarity.

(e) The ring (Pl. IVa)

The ring found at the same time as the Anglo-Saxon objects may be dated to the fifteenth or sixteenth century, and is of a type likely to have been worn by a member of the lesser gentry or clergy. It exhibits motifs common to signet, love and devotional rings of the period[58].

(f) The burials

Although the Archaeological Journal's description of the burials is far from satisfactory, it does seem worth exploring some of the hypotheses which could explain the wording of the report. Without verifiable evidence, any conclusions must be tentative. There are two interrelated problems to solve: if it is accepted that there was a single rich burial separate from the circle of skeletons, then what was the nature of that burial, and what was the reason for the circle of burials? It is easiest to begin with the latter.

The number of skeletons uncovered is unknown. The 1970 excavation accounted for a minimum of four persons, and "several" implies that there was not a large number. Perhaps up to ten bodies would be a reasonable estimate. They were said to have been arranged in a circle with their heads outwards, that is in a radial layout, though it is not clear whether they formed a complete circle or only an arc of one.

Radial burials are rare, and the fact that most were excavated before the Second World War might cast doubt on their identification. There are only two cases where radial burials were found in quite definite Anglo-Saxon contexts. Two concentric circles of bodies were found at Tickford Park Estate, Newport Pagnell (Bucks)[59], the grave-goods accompanying the individual burials dating from about 500 A.D. Probably the best recorded example of all comes from the Upper Thames valley itself, from the seventh-century cemetery at Stanton Harcourt[60] where the graves were placed round the eastern arc of the ditch of a prehistoric round barrow. Four seventh-century burials around the rim of Riley's barrow 17 at Standlake (Oxon), just west of Stanton Harcourt, are less convincing as part of a circle[61]. The other English sites of which I know have no datable associations. Five to seven skeletons, radiating from a common centre, were found by B. H. Cunnington at Great Bedwyn (Wilts), where other skeletons had been previously discovered[62]. No concrete information has survived about "two cases of bodies being in a circle" at Shoeburyness (Essex)[63], nor about the ten to twelve skeletons found before 1965 in a "clock" formation at Swanage (Dorset)[64]; whilst the Royal Commission on Historical Monuments's attribution of a number of burials found arranged in a circle at Peterborough (Northants) to the Roman period seems to have little justification[65]. On the continent, skeletons were found placed round the edge of small circular ditches in the large "Reihengräberfeld" at Vendhuile, Dépt. Aisne[66]. Radial burials are also reported from early Christian sites in the Celtic West, though the identification is not always certain: the most frequently cited example, Kilnasaggart (Co. Armagh) has recently been shown not to have been radial at all[67]. One phase in the use of a cemetery at Arfryn, on Anglesey, is characterised by rows of approximately west to east burials curving slightly towards a central feature, probably some sort of grave or grave-shrine, but the arrangement was not radial in the sense of spokes of a wheel[68].

Apart from their radial layout, these cemeteries have little in common, though the datable examples do all fall within the Dark Ages. The burials in any one cemetery do seem to conform to a single alignment, either head or feet to the centre, but there appears to have been no significance in the choice. It is difficult, therefore, to know why radial layout was used. Mr. White suggests that for the Celtic sites which he has examined it is nearly always a question of local geography, the use of a constricted circular area, frequently a small island or hillock, for a cemetery.

In Anglo-Saxon contexts a pre-existing barrow mound would best provide similar circumstances. Although cemeteries in or associated with barrows are quite common, only Stanton Harcourt employed a true radial layout. If the plan is correct, Barrow C 38 at Driffield (Yorks, E. R.)[69] also has some radial burials, in several concentric circles, but there is no uniformity in alignment and there are some definite exceptions to the layout, which makes it an uncertain example. Stanton Harcourt does suggest an obvious method of achieving a circle of burials, namely by placing them round the edge of a barrow.

Is it possible that the burials at Cuddesdon were also placed round a barrow? Even if it is accepted that the single rich grave-assemblage was found near the skeletons, there is no evidence that it was found in the centre of the circle. Given the nature of the Cuddesdon grave-goods, however, burial under a barrow mound would not be surprising, since the graves in which the Cuddesdon assemblage finds its best parallels were mostly barrow-burials. The hill-top at Cuddesdon with its extensive views towards the Chilterns and the Thames valley is a typical situation for a barrow. The suggestion that the grave had been robbed might explain why parish records make no mention of a barrow: it need never have been a very large mound[70] and could have been easily levelled by grave-robbers. The existence of a rich barrow-burial at Cuddesdon is a feasible hypothesis, and it provides the most reasonable explanation of the circle of skeletons, but it poses fresh questions about the nature of the central burial and the circumstances which produced the encircling burials.

It would appear that the body from the central grave was not found. There are several possible answers. It may be thought that there was no body at all, since a number of other rich graves also apparently lacked a body, for example Broomfield, Coombe Bissett (Wilts)[71] and both the ship-burials at Sutton Hoo. These sites were excavated well before the present day and with insufficient expertise, so that results obtained from them cannot be accepted without reserve. The latest chemical tests on the material from Sutton Hoo mound 1 suggest that a body could have been present[72], whilst mound 2 had clearly been ransacked[73]. That there was no body at Cuddesdon seems unlikely.

There are good arguments for the burial being either a cremation or a robbed-out inhumation. Cremated bones could easily have escaped recognition. It is possible that these were originally placed in the bucket, with the unburnt grave-goods deposited by its side. The use of a bronze bowl as a cinerary receptacle and the deposition of unburnt grave-goods had some currency in the late sixth and early seventh centuries: it has been observed at Coombe[74], Loveden Hill (Lincs) and Sutton Hoo mound 3.

Alternatively there was an inhumation. Given the fine condition in which bone survives on the site, it is improbable that an inhumation would have been missed, unless the workmen struck only part of a burial chamber, and, failing to recognise the grave-fill for what it was, did not reach the body. If the circle of skeletons was in fact an arc, and only a segment of the former barrow was excavated, it would have been possible to uncover only a fraction of the grave. No personal jewellery, which might indicate the presence of a clothed body, was recorded as found. On the other hand, swords were generally placed by the side of the corpse or in some central position[75]. However, if the grave had been robbed the absence of the skeleton and of personal jewellery becomes explicable[76].

There remain the questions of the date of the circle of burials and the reason for them. There is no definite evidence for their date. The assumption that they are Anglo-Saxon is based on their apparent relationship to the principal grave, and the fact that datable radial cemeteries are of Dark Age date. If the bronze lace-tag found amongst the scatter of small bones in the 1970 excavation reflected an original association it might provide more certain evidence; and if a medieval date is preferred for the tag, then it might be thought that the occurrence of the late medieval ring was more than a coincidence, and that both objects were associated with the burials. However, I know of no radial burial which is definitely medieval and there is no evidence that the Cuddesdon churchyard extended in this direction (the church is some 130 metres south-east of the site). Since neither the date nor the association of the lace-tag is certain it is best removed from the argument[77]. A Saxon date for the skeletons remains the most likely.

The "family" or "community" character of the skeletons found in 1970 would suggest that the graves belonged to members of a nearby settlement who had died naturally and were buried around a pre-existing barrow mound, perhaps because it was known to be a burial of a leader of their folk, or because the existence of one burial signified an area suitable to receive the dead. This would be acceptable but for yet another problematic statement in the 1847 report: the skeletons were lying on their faces with their legs crossed. Prone burial is far from normal among the Anglo-Saxons. For every hundred burials in an average cemetery, perhaps one or two might be prone, but the apparent uniformity of the Cuddesdon burials is unique. When the uncommon radial arrangement is also taken into account, these skeletons appear even less like a normal cemetery, and an alternative explanation is required. Both the prone position and the crossed legs, which might indicate that they had been originally tied, seem to suggest something more sinister than natural death. Could they have been deliberately put to death?

One solution may be raised only to be dismissed. "Execution" cemeteries, mostly dating from the middle to late Saxon period onwards, were often associated with isolated hill-tops and particularly with barrows or ditches[78]. They have other common features: the burials are usually haphazard or bunched together in heaps; a large proportion of the skeletons are decapitated and their hands are tied; they are normally adult males, and are usually buried in their clothes, so that small items such as buckles, rings, strap-tags and knives survive; finally, the sites are often associated with a hundred meeting-place, a market or major highway. The Cuddesdon cemetery fails to conform on nearly all these points.

Another possibility is sacrifice. This may seem an audacious suggestion, since the complete absence of any reference to it by the early Christian missionaries is a strong argument against its occurrence in England. Yet it was not unknown to the Germanic world. Procopius described how the Franks under Theudebert sacrificed Ostrogothic women and children at Pavia in 539 as the first fruits of war, retaining, he wrote, their barbarian customs despite their Christianity[79]; and Professor Chaney has argued that a number of English references reflect similar cases of human sacrifice to Woden[80]. There are various possible types of sacrifice associated with a grave. The number of bodies at Cuddesdon rules out suttee-type sacrifice, for which there is the best evidence: sacrifice of a man's wife, or a slave girl instead of his wife, is recorded historically amongst the Rus[81], as well as in Scandinavian sagas[82], and amongst the non-Germanic Wends[83]; in Anglo-Saxon contexts there are examples of double-burials which might parallel these practices; the possible connection between such a custom, cremation and Odin-worship in Scandinavia may be repeated at Coombe[84]. But the Cuddesdon burials were more likely to have been slaves or captives; the best instance of the sacrifice of household slaves is in the account of Sigurðr's funeral pyre in Sigurðarkviða hin Skamma[85].

At what date could such a sacrifice have been made? If it was at a later date than the central burial, then it is a possibility that it was made in bad times to regain the "luck" of a prosperous ruler[86] - Wessex did not become officially Christian until 635, and was troubled by apostasy and political upheavals in the later 640s, 670s and 680s - but there is no evidence for such a custom. Sacrifice on the occasion of the burial is more likely, being closer to the attested instances. It does not seem out of the question at Cuddesdon, particularly in association with the grave of a high-ranking man, though the manner and meaning of the rite would remain obscure.

SUMMARY

It is not possible to date precisely any of the Anglo-Saxon objects found in 1847 at Cuddesdon, but together they suggest that the burial took place some time during the early seventh century. The strong links between it and the group of "princely" burials have been sufficiently emphasised, and justify the description of Cuddesdon as "princely". The Cuddesdon burial apparently lacked the quantity of objects found in the others[87], but it was the equal of all but the great ship-burial in quality; and in the possession of objects rare or unique in the Germanic world, it shared in a distinctive feature of these "princely" graves. In comparison with other burials in the Upper Thames region, there is no doubt about its outstanding nature.

II. DORCHESTER-ON-THAMES

Dorchester-on-Thames lies on a gravel terrace between the confluence of the Rivers Thames and Thame, some five miles to the south of Cuddesdon. Much of the archaeological evidence for settlement there is unpublished, and a full understanding of its history must await such a publication. During the Roman period Dorchester was a small town, which served as a centre for this part of the Thames Valley. It had a long life, and its apparent final protection by Germanic soldiers is well known[88]. Recent excavations are making it clear that at least by the sixth century there was fairly extensive Saxon settlement within the old Roman town, and it is probable that there was an inhumation cemetery of this period just to the north-west of the town at Bishop's Court House[89]. Although the implications of this apparent continuity will need thorough examination, the fact that Dorchester was already occupied by a considerable body of Saxons provides the background to its use in the early seventh century as the ecclesiastical centre, at least, of Wessex, and to the archaeological evidence for the existence there of a very rich settlement. This evidence consists of a number of gold finds, which in comparison with sparse gold finds elsewhere in the Upper Thames region points to Dorchester as a centre of wealth during the early seventh century.

THE COINS[90]

In 1823 J. J. Skelton illustrated three gold coins found somewhere in Dorchester[91]. Two were solidi, one of Valentinian I (364-375) and the other a light-weight issue of Mauricius Tiberius (582-602)[92], both types popular for mounting as pendants, especially in the seventh century, which would account for the survival of the former until that century. The third was a runic early Anglo-Saxon gold coin probably contemporary with the Crondall (Hants) hoard, that is about 640-650[93]. It is impossible to know whether these coins came from graves or from one or more hoards or whether they were stray finds.

THE PYRAMIDAL STUD (Pl. IVb and Fig. 3b)

In 1776 a pyramidal stud was found in the course of hedge digging somewhere in Dorchester, and on November 28 of that year a Mr. Barrington exhibited it to the Society of Antiquaries of London. The stud has since been lost, and the only record of it survives in the Society's Minute Book, vol. XV, p. 40[94]. The description and the coloured sketch pasted on to the margin seem sufficiently reliable to permit some archaeological comment[95].

It had four trapezoidal sides, a base about 1" (2.5cm) square, and a truncated top about 3/10" (0.8cm) square; it was some 7/10" (1.8cm) high. The sketch in the Minute Book makes the base less than an inch square, but otherwise accords accurately with the given measurements. The stud was made of gold and had two apertures in its base, thought to have been for a catch or means of attachment. These "apertures" presumably represent the spaces on either side of the narrow bar found on other pyramid studs, through which a strap could be threaded[96]. The top of the stud was inlaid with a single garnet and the sides decorated with elaborate cloisonné. In the sketch some of the cells are coloured red, as for garnets, but others are blank. The symmetry of blank cells may suggest an attempt to clarify the design rather than to show missing garnets. It is possible that they represent settings of different substances - white shell was used on the Coombe Bissett studs - but the text makes no mention of settings other than garnet. It is unlikely that they were capped with gold in the "lidded-cell" technique, used on the purse-lid and shoulder clasps from Sutton Hoo; on those the lidded cells tend to be large and irregular, quite unlike the cell-work on the Dorchester stud.

There is a border around the central field of the stud, widest along the base and narrowest down the sides. Three square garnets occupy the upper border, and five rectangular cells fill the lateral borders. The basal border is more complicated: a trapezoidal cell, subdivided into smaller units, occupies the left-hand corner; four half-mushroom cells lying on their sides, with four vertical bars linking each mushroom to the upper edge of the border, fill the centre of the panel; the cellwork in the right-hand corner is unclear; it might have been intended as a fifth half-mushroom, or as a sub-divided trapezoidal cell, as in the left-hand corner. The central field contains two major motifs: the upper part is occupied by four interlocked mushroom cells, their stalks towards the centre; below, an inverted "V" separates two mushroom cells, each standing above an inverted T-cell. This pattern was presumably identical on all four sides of the stud.

The precise function of studs such as the Dorchester one is not certain, but they seem to have been used either to ornament or to adjust straps on the scabbard or harness of swords[97]. They are found mainly in seventh-century sword-graves on the continent and, less frequently, in England. Most of them are made of iron or bronze, but the Dorchester stud belongs to a select group made from gold. The magnificent pair from the Sutton Hoo ship-burial[98] and one from the west mound at Old Uppsala[99] in Sweden are decorated purely with cloisonné work like the Dorchester stud; the one from Broomfield has a single garnet set in each face, bordered with herring-bone filigree[100]; and two, from Dalmeny, just west of Edinburgh[101], and Etzinge, in Friesland[102], are decorated primarily with filigree, but have simple settings of garnets in each face and on the top. The first two sites have definitely royal associations[103], and I have suggested that, by implication, graves such as Broomfield represent only a slightly less exalted social rank. The find-contexts for the last two examples, which are technically much less impressive than the others, are uncertain: the Etzinge stud came from a terp site, whilst the context of the one from Dalmeny is unknown. In view of its parallels, the Dorchester stud most probably came from a grave, but it is impossible to prove this. However, its parallels also indicate that the original owner was a man of very exalted status, which is the most significant point.

The relationship of the Dorchester stud with the school of jewellery represented in the Sutton Hoo ship-burial reinforces such a view. Among the major characteristics of this school is the intensive use of the mush-room cell and its employment in complex regular motifs, which has been used, with other parallels in jewellery technique, to suggest that a number of objects were made in the same workshop or under its direct influence[104].

The techniques used on the Dorchester stud cannot be examined, and comment must be confined to the decoration. The motif of four interlocked mushroom-cells has no exact parallel in the Sutton Hoo material; the closest is the motif of two mushroom cells and two arrowhead cells, found on the pseudo-buckle and the plate of the strap-distributor[105] (Fig. 3d). This occurs on three other objects: the Wilton Cross[106] (Fig. 3g), the ornament in Tongres Cathedral treasury[107] (Fig. 3e), and the outer frame of the composite disc set into the Egbert reliquary shrine at Trier[108] (Fig. 3f). On the last this motif interlocks with the motif of four mushroom cells used on the Dorchester stud, the two motifs sharing, so to speak, their lateral mushroom cells. Bruce-Mitford's confident identification of the Wilton Cross and the Tongres ornament as products of the Sutton Hoo workshop has remained unquestioned; he was less certain about the Egbert shrine disc on account of its green glass inlays and unusual cross-section, but thought that an East Anglian origin of somewhat later date was still most probable[109]. The oval profile and the cross-section are indeed distinct features, but unusual inlays are also found on the Tongres ornament, alternate garnet and amethyst borders, and large raised amethysts and onyx(?) set in the upper panel; this feature, therefore, is not wholly alien to the workshop[110]. If the Egbert shrine disc was made in East Anglia, then it was surely at the Sutton Hoo workshop, since it is difficult to imagine that any but the royal house could have patronised such costly art-work. If it was made elsewhere, even on the continent, it is still likely that the craftsman had a very close link with the Sutton Hoo workshop.

The occurrence of the mushroom cell is by itself no proof of a link with Sutton Hoo; on continental cloisonné jewellery it appears rarely, the number of cells employed is low and the pattern often asymmetrical, a far cry from the Sutton Hoo workshop[111]. By contrast, the mushroom cell was frequently copied from the second quarter of the seventh century onwards in silver-inlaid iron belt-equipment[112], often in the precise motif of the four interlocked cells, though the treatment is usually simple and clumsy. On present evidence, it is difficult to think that this motif was copied from continental jewellery, since there is a remarkable shortage of other exempla; one may suspect that once introduced into the new medium it continued without further reference to the originals. It cannot in any case be considered evidence for the existence on the continent of a workshop rivalling Sutton Hoo.

The intensive use of mushroom cells, as well as the motif of four interlocked cells, may, then, be grounds for a direct link between the Dorchester stud and the Sutton Hoo workshop. The general appearance of the stud lends support to this idea: the intricate all-over pattern, involving a considerable number of cells within such a confined space, is a hallmark of the cloisonné jewellery from the ship-burial. Although the Sutton Hoo pyramidal studs employ far more complicated techniques than are used on the Dorchester stud, there is a basic similarity in their plan of single square setting on the top of the truncated pyramid and borders of different widths around a central complex pattern.

The only feature which might suggest that the Dorchester stud was made by a craftsman imperfectly trained in the skills of the Sutton Hoo workshop is the uneven quality of the lower border. The drawing of the half-mushroom cells in the Minute Book sketch appears particularly slipshod, and may be inaccurate; if it is not, then the cellwork is not quite regular, breaking down completely at the right-hand corner. The half-mushroom cell border is found at Sutton Hoo, on the edge of the large cloisonné buckle, the mushrooms containing an extra step in their profile (Fig. 3c); but it was often copied on other items, for which there is no evidence to suggest an association with the workshop, such as the Wye Down pendant, which has lost its settings[113].

There is, then, a strong possibility that the Dorchester pyramidal stud was made in the so-called Sutton Hoo workshop, though the slight discrepancies between it and the items actually found in the ship-burial may indicate that it was made at a later date or by a less gifted jeweller. There is an equal possibility that it was made elsewhere, though by a man closely connected with, and probably trained at the Sutton Hoo workshop. The only objection to its manufacture in the Upper Thames valley is the unreliable negative evidence that no other object has been found there which could be attributed to such a workshop. However, the two gold solidi from Dorchester could have been originally part of a jeweller's working-stock, and if so, would be evidence for a craftsman working there under a very rich patron.

Its date of manufacture was probably within the second quarter of the seventh century. The gold and garnet jewellery in the Sutton Hoo ship-burial is among the latest items in the assemblage, and might have been made in the decade before 625; the Dorchester stud might have been made at a slightly later date. If the stud did come from a burial, then it was probably almost contemporary with the one at Cuddesdon.

III. HISTORICAL SUMMARY

The identification of one likely and one possible "princely" burial close to the heart of Saxon settlement in the Upper Thames valley adds a potent-ially important detail to the meagre evidence for an early Saxon political centre there.

There can be little doubt that, during the period in which these burials must have taken place, the Upper Thames valley was part of the kingdom of Wessex. The region is not mentioned in the historical records until the second half of the sixth century, when, in a series of far-ranging military expeditions, Ceawlin and his associates are said to have captured a number of settlements in and around the valley. Although the Upper Thames valley appears as the natural geographical centre of these conquests, there is no explicit indication that the West Saxon kings had established a royal centre there until about 635, when Dorchester-on-Thames was chosen as the seat of their first bishop. That the Upper Thames valley was the centre for Ceawlin's, and some of his successors', activities, would seem logical; and in view of the known imbalance in the archaeological evidence for settle-ment between north and south Wessex, the apparently distinct elements within the West Saxon genealogy, and the problems of a satisfactory inter-pretation of political events under Ceawlin, this may have been an original West Saxon centre[114]. By the late 640s Mercian designs on the Upper Thames valley were threatening West Saxon security; the West Saxon kings withdrew to the Hampshire/Wiltshire area and the see at Dorchester-on-Thames was abandoned, at the latest, by the 660s. Their later direction of expansion was westwards.

The placing of a West Saxon royal centre in the Upper Thames valley may find further support in the recognition of a number of sites with royal associations. The connection between _villae regales_ and hundred centres and old minsters or early monasteries seems to be one indication of a very early origin for some royal estates, for example Abingdon in Berkshire, and Headington and Bensington in Oxfordshire[115]. Of these the great Domesday royal manor of Bensington probably has the best claim to have been an early seventh century royal estate: it had the rare distinction to be named in the _Anglo-Saxon Chronicle_ annal s. a. 571; it was important enough to have another battle fought over it in 777 (s. a. 779); and in 887 it was specifically named as a royal vill[116].

Dorchester-on-Thames is not recorded as a royal vill: it was confirmed in ecclesiastical possession in the late ninth century when the Mercian see at Leicester was transferred to Dorchester. Its probable assessment at a hundred hides, and its association with Thame and Banbury in a triple hundred may reflect an earlier centre of administration[117], but the most compelling argument for its having been an early West Saxon royal centre is its choice as the first diocesan seat: Bede makes it clear that the successful spread of Christianity depended on a very close association between missionaries and kings. The presence of a man of "princely" status at Dorchester would be quite consistent both with its implied historical function and the archaeological indications that it was a centre of wealth.

The choice of Cuddesdon as the site of a "princely" burial requires a different explanation. In the tenth century King Edwy granted the estate to one of his thegns[118]. It included the present civil parish of Wheatley, in which a cemetery, datable from about the early sixth to the early seventh, has been excavated[119]. This cemetery has two features of some relevance: it marks almost the only early Saxon settlement known in the area between the Chilterns, the Cherwell, the Thames, and the group of cemeteries south-west of Aylesbury (Bucks); the pair of jeweller's scale-pans found in a woman's grave and two weights, one from a grave, the other a stray find, imply that members of the community had some connection, even if at second-hand, with the working of precious metals[120]. Apart from this settlement, the area, which was probably wooded or waste land (the later royal hunting forest of Shotover lay just to the north-west), was suitably remote for a pagan barrow-burial, especially if it was accompanied by grisly rituals; the elevated site, which has already been noted as typical of barrow-burials, was conveniently separated from Wheatley by a deep wooded valley[121]. In view of the Wheatley settlement, one does wonder whether the tenth-century estate had a much earlier origin as a unit of land to be granted out by the king, or conceivably as a royal possession itself[122]. If so, it would provide a plausible reason why Cuddesdon was chosen for a "princely" burial.

The place-name "Cuddesdon" provides an occasion for speculation on the historical associations of the burial. In the 956 charter Cuddesdon occurs as Cuþenes dune, using the personal form *Cūðen in its genitive singular inflected form[123]. The same name with the suffix hlæw (barrow-mound) occurs at Cutteslowe (Oxon), where a barrow is known to have existed. Dr. Myres has postulated that Cutteslowe was the burial mound of the Cutha killed at Fethanleag in 584, taking note of the fact that the Cūð-proto-theme was a dominant form among the West Saxon dynasty[124]. The identification cannot be proved, since the barrow was demolished in 1261, and it is equally possible that it had been a prehistoric long or round barrow[125]. Another cudan hlæwe is known in the charter boundary dated 995 for Cuxham in east Oxfordshire[126], and the Cutha commemorated probably also gave his name to a field called Cuddington at the north-west corner of Watlington parish, close to its junction with Cuxham, which is first recorded c. 1220 as Cudendone, using the -dun (hill) suffix as in Cuddesdon[127]. There is one other Cūð-name in the area, Cuddington, a parish just in Buckinghamshire, recorded c. 1120 as Cudintuna[128], an -ing[4] formation which, though not as early in origin as other -ingas or inga forms, nevertheless uses a personal name in some associative way with a settlement[129].

The early West Saxon dynasty's personal names are rather interesting: not only were they strictly c-alliterative until the appearance of Aescwine about 675, but from about 550 to 680 Cūð- was the most consistently used prototheme. A glance at the genealogy shows two, if not three, Cuthas, a

32

Cuthwine, Cuthwulf, Cuthgils, Cuthred, and Cuthburgh, a feminine form. C-alliteration is found in the Mercian dynasty, but principally among the ancestors of King Ceolwulf (821-823), and this might have been the result of intermarriage with West Saxons.

The question is whether the use of the same prototheme proves a link between the place-names and the West Saxon dynasty. Cūð- prototheme place-names are virtually confined to England south-west of a line from Thanet to the Wirral (Fig. 4)[130], occurring more frequently in Gloucestershire, Worcestershire, Oxfordshire, Surrey, west Sussex and east Kent, and less so in Wessex south of the Thames. Although much of the area of dense distribution was ruled or influenced by Wessex, the correlation is not precise. It is also uncertain whether place-names based on personal names were the result of one man giving his name to a number of places within a locality, or the name being common to several men who each gave their name to a settlement. No doubt a combination of both factors was involved, but the former might seem more likely where there is a concentration of place-names, as in the Oxford area.

Thus, a definite association between Cūð- place-names and the Wessex dynasty cannot be demonstrated, but for a concentrated group like those of the Oxford area it remains something of a probability, and the occurrence of one of them at the site of a probable "princely" burial may be more than a coincidence.

If there was a connection between the "princely" burial at Cuddesdon and a member of the West Saxon dynasty in the Upper Thames, he remains unknown. In searching for the origin of the shire system, Professor H. M. Chadwick drew attention to the many examples of "princes" or sub-kings within the kingdom of Wessex[131]. There are references to kings whose genealogical relation to the ruling dynasty is unknown, (e.g. the sub-king Cissa, who was the first to grant land to Abingdon Abbey), to unnamed kings, like the five, possibly sub-kings of the more northerly provinces of Wessex, killed by King Edwin of Northumbria in 626, and there are many names in the West Saxon genealogies whose political role has not been recorded, but who might be expected to have ranked as sub-kings. The

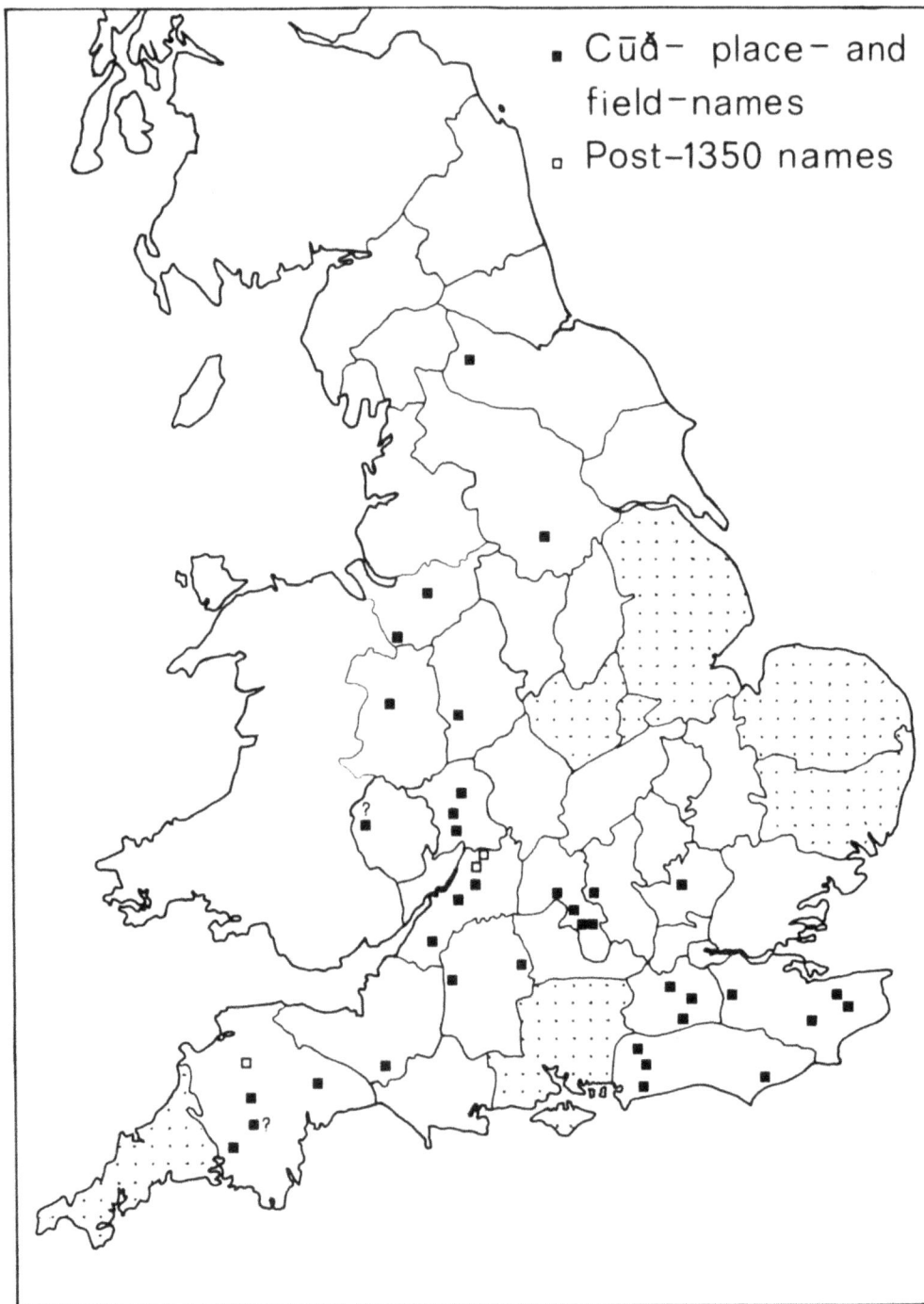

FIG. 4 – Provisional distribution map of Cūð - prototheme place-names based on counties; stippled counties are those for which no published place-name survey is available; a question mark by a site indicates that its location is uncertain.

status and function of these _subreguli_ cannot be closely defined, but their position within the ruling hierarchy may link them with burials evaluated on archaeological grounds as "princely".

The archaeological grounds for associating Cuddesdon with a West Saxon prince are undeniably slender. It is worth remembering that neither this burial nor the material from Dorchester included any object which could link them culturally with the Upper Thames; on the contrary, it was argued that the goods were typical of high-ranking burials elsewhere. The historical records for the seventh century leave no doubt about the intimate connections between various kingdoms, and the mobility of both persons and objects within this upper class: marriage alliances, baptismal sponsorships and the initiation or reward of warrior-retainers would all involve the exchange of gifts and the movement of people to alien courts. Another feature of the period was the exiling of high-ranking men, who would take with them their own followers, and possibly their own jeweller[132]. This brings to mind the apparently East Anglian affinities of the Dorchester stud, especially since King Cenwalh of Wessex himself, who was forced into exile between 645 and 648, took refuge at the court of Anna of East Anglia, suggesting that there were close links of friendship pre-existing between the two kingdoms.

The difficulty of establishing such historical details should not, however, be allowed to obscure the importance of the identification of "princely" material at Cuddesdon and Dorchester-on-Thames, and the archaeological evidence which this provides for an early centre of royal power in the Upper Thames valley.

October 1972

Institute of Archaeology,
Oxford

APPENDIX I: THE HUMAN BONE MATERIAL FOUND AT CUDDESDON IN 1970

by ANNA S. KILNER and BRIGID E. CAMPBELL

The majority of the human bone material was excavated from the upper fill-ing of the nineteenth-century sewer-trench, most of the large bones being in one group at the junction of the west end of Trench VII and Trench I. Small bones were more scattered, and a few were found in other trenches, mainly II and IV, which were both close to the sewer-trench. The bones were all disarticulated, intermixed and out of their original context; their partially fragmentary state has made identification in some cases difficult.

Animal bones, many of which had been sawn or cooked, were found scattered over the entire excavated area. A sawn long bone of a young pig and a sawn head of a bovine rib were among the main pile of human bone, which makes it possible that some were originally associated with the human bones, though it is more likely that they were rubbish from the epis-copal kitchens.

All the human bone is in extremely good condition, and most is coloured by an orangy patina, distinguishing it from the mainly grey or white animal bone. The patina was the result, no doubt, of the bones having lain in the orangy-yellow subsoil. The human bones completely lack any ante-mortem pathology.

A minimum of four bodies can be reconstructed from the bones, which are described under the individual to whom they most probably belonged. Bones which cannot be ascribed to any particular skeleton are added at the end. The number of the trench in which each bone was found is put in brack-ets. The estimation of stature has been done for each bone individually according to the formulae of Trotter and Gleser[133]. For the adult male the result from the two leg bones together is the same as from each individually, but the humerus gives a much higher reading. The dental formulae used are those advocated by Dr. Brothwell[134]: a number with a diagonal stroke above or below it (1) signifies that the tooth is missing, but the socket is present; a number with a circle (1) signifies that a tooth is in the process of erupting.

1. Child, aged between eight years and puberty, sex unknown.

   <u>1st sacral vertebra</u> (VII).

2. Female, aged about twenty years; stature estimated from right humerus as 1.557m. (4' 11¾").

   <u>Mandible</u> (VII); <u>Maxilla</u> (VII): palatal length, 0.040m., palatal breadth, 0.038m.; <u>Left parietal bone</u> (VII); <u>Left zygomatic bone</u> (VII); <u>12th thoracic vertebra</u> (VII); <u>Lumbar vertebra</u> (II); <u>Pelvis</u> (VII): general loss of epiphyseal margins from left half; <u>Right humerus</u> (VII); <u>Left radius</u> (VII): an exceptionally puny bone, greyish in colour, and missing its lower distal epiphysis; <u>Head and upper shaft of right femur</u> (VII); <u>Distal end of left femur</u> (VII).

   <u>Dentition</u>: Signs of dental attrition consonant with age.

   ```
   /   / / / / / / / / /   /
   8 7 6 5 4 3 2 1 1 2 3 4 5 6 7 8
   8 7 6 5 4 3 2 1 1 2 3 4 5 6 7 8
   0           / /           0
   ```

3. Female, adult; stature estimated as 1.570m. (5' 2").

   <u>Right femur</u> (VII): minimal early arthritic change, length 0.413m.

4. Male, adult, probably in late middle age.

   <u>Left clavicle</u> (VII); <u>Left scapula</u> (VII); <u>Left half of pelvis</u> (VII): hole through ilium produced by some artefact (? a nineteenth-century pick-axe !); sciatic notch angle, 50°; <u>Right acetabulum, half of ilium and half of superior pubic ramus</u> (VII); <u>Fragment of ilium with auricular surface</u> (VII); <u>Sacrum</u> (VII); <u>Right humerus</u> (VII): maximum length 0.358m., giving an estimated stature of 1.820m (6' 1½"); <u>Proximal half of right ulna</u> (VII): articulates with humerus; <u>Right femur</u> (VII) and <u>Medial condyle</u> (I): slight arthritic change to head; length, 0.480m., giving an estimated stature of 1.770m. (5' 9¾"); <u>Head and upper shaft of left femur</u> (VII): minimal arthritic changes; <u>Left tibia</u> (VII): length 0.392m., giving an estimated stature of 1.770m (5' 9¾"); <u>Midshaft of tibia and two fragments from same bone</u> (VII).

Unattributed bones

   <u>Right rib</u> (I): 3rd to 10th; <u>? Occipital condyle</u> (VII); <u>Femoral condyle</u>

(II); Proximal phalanx of left thumb (VII): from an adult, but very small, ? female; Right talus (VII): from an adult; Right cuboid bone (VII); 4th metatarsal of right foot (VII): articulates with cuboid bone; ? from an adult; 1st metatarsal (? right) (VII): from an adult; Two fragments of tarsal bones (VII); Proximal phalanx of toe (IV); Small proximal phalanx of finger or toe (VII): from an adult; Fragment of ? digital shaft (VIII); one unidentifiable human fragment (II).

BIBLIOGRAPHY

Åberg 1926	N. Åberg, The Anglo-Saxons in England (Cambridge 1926).
Akerman 1855	J. Y. Akerman, Remains of Pagan Saxondom (London 1855).
Alcock 1971	L. Alcock, Arthur's Britain (London 1971)
Arne and Stolpe 1927	T. J. Arne and H. Stolpe, La Nécropole de Vendel (Stockholm 1927)
Arwidsson 1942	G. Arwidsson, Die Gräberfunde von Valsgärde I (Uppsala 1942).
Baldwin Brown 1915	G. Baldwin Brown, The Arts in Early England IV (London 1915).
Birch	Cartularium Saxonicum I-III, ed. W. de G. Birch (London 1885-1893).
Biddle 1971	M. Biddle, 'Archaeology and the beginnings of English society', in England Before the Conquest: Studies in primary sources presented to Dorothy Whitelock, ed. P. Clemoes and K. Hughes (Cambridge 1971), 391-408.
Biddle et al. 1968	M. Biddle, the late Mrs. H. T. Lambrick and J. N. L. Myres, 'The early history of Abingdon, Berkshire, and its abbey', Medieval Archaeology, XII, 1968, 26-69.
Brothwell 1965	D. R. Brothwell, Digging up Bones (London 1965).
Bruce-Mitford 1948	R. L. S. Bruce-Mitford, 'Saxon Rendlesham', Proceedings of the Suffolk Institute of Archaeology, XXIV, 1948, 228-251.
" " 1949	R. L. S. Bruce-Mitford, 'The Sutton Hoo ship-burial', Proceedings of the Suffolk Institute of Archaeology, XXV, 1949, 1-78.
" " 1952	R. L. S. Bruce-Mitford, 'The Snape boat-grave', Proceedings of the Suffolk Institute of Archaeology, XXVI, 1952, 1-26.
" " 1954	R. L. S. Bruce-Mitford, 'Gold and silver cloisonné buckle from Wynaldum, Friesland', 120ste Verslag van het Fries Genootschnap van Geschied-, Oudheid-, en Taalhunde Te Leeuwarden, 1954, 16-17.
" " 1964	R. L. S. Bruce-Mitford, 'Excavations at Sutton Hoo in 1938', Proceedings of the Suffolk Institute of Archaeology, XXX, 1964, 1-43.

Bruce-Mitford 1970	R. L. S. and M. Bruce-Mitford, 'The Sutton Hoo Lyre, Beowulf, and the origins of the frame harp', Antiquity, XLIV, 1970, 7-13.
" " 1972	R. L. S. Bruce-Mitford, The Sutton Hoo ship-burial: a Handbook, 2nd edition (London 1972).
Cam 1932	H. M. Cam, 'Manerium cum hundredo: the hundred and the hundredal manor', English Historical Review, XLVII, 1932, 353-376.
" 1933	H. M. Cam, 'Early groups of hundreds', in Historical Essays in honour of James Tait, ed. J. G. Edwards et al. (Manchester 1933), 13-25.
Cam and Crawford 1935	H. M. Cam and O. G. S. Crawford, 'The Hoga of Cutteslowe', Antiquity, IX, 1935, 96-98.
Chadwick 1905	H. M. Chadwick, Studies on Anglo-Saxon Institutions (Cambridge 1905).
Chaney 1970	W. A. Chaney, The Cult of Kingship in Anglo-Saxon England (Manchester 1970).
Cole 1959	J. C. Cole, 'The building of the second palace at Cuddesdon', Oxoniensia, XXIV, 1959, 49-69.
Crowfoot and Hawkes 1967	E. Crowfoot and S. C. Hawkes, 'Early Anglo-Saxon Gold Braids', Medieval Archaeology, XI, 1967, 42-86.
Dalton 1912	O. M. Dalton, Catalogue of the finger-rings in the British Museum (London 1912).
de Baye 1893	J. de Baye, Industrial Arts of the Anglo-Saxons (London 1893).
de Palol Salellas	P. de Palol Salellas, Bronces hispanovisigodos de origen Mediterráneo I: Jarritos y patenos litúrgicos (Barcelona 1950).
Douglas 1793	J. Douglas, Nenia Britannica (London 1793).
Ellis 1943	H. R. Ellis, The Road to Hel (Cambridge 1943)
Ellis Davidson 1962	H. R. Ellis Davidson, The Sword in Anglo-Saxon England (Oxford 1962).
Ellis Davidson and Webster 1967	H. R. Ellis Davidson and L. Webster, 'The Anglo-Saxon burial at Coombe (Woodnesborough), Kent', Medieval Archaeology, XI, 1967, 1-41.
Emery 1938	W. B. Emery, The Royal Tombs at Ballana and Qustal (Cairo 1938).
EPNS	English Place-Name Society II, Buckinghamshire (Cambridge 1925), XXIII, Oxfordshire (Cambridge 1953).

Evison 1963	V. I. Evison, 'Sugar-loaf shield bosses', Antiquaries Journal, XLIII, 1963, 38-96.
" 1967	V. I. Evison, 'The Dover ring-sword and other sword rings and beads', Archaeologia, CI, 1967, 63-118.
Fleury 1877	E. Fleury, Antiquités et monuments du Dépt. de l'Aisne II (Paris 1877).
Frere 1962	S. S. Frere, 'Excavations at Dorchester-on-Thames, 1962', Archaeological Journal, CXIX, 1962, 114-149.
" 1966	S. S. Frere, 'The end of towns in Roman Britain', in The Civitas Capitals of Roman Britain, ed. J. S. Wacher (Leicester 1966), 87-100.
Fuchs and Werner 1950	S. Fuchs and J. Werner, Die Langobardischen Fibeln aus Italien (Berlin 1950).
Harden 1956	D. B. Harden, 'Glass vessels in Britain and Ireland, A. D. 400-1000', in Dark Age Britain, Studies presented to E. T. Leeds, ed. D. B. Harden (London 1956), 133-167.
Harden and Treweeks 1945	D. B. Harden and R. C. Treweeks, 'Excavations at Stanton Harcourt, Oxon., 1940, II', Oxoniensia, X, 1945, 33-41.
Hawkes 1962-3	S. C. Hawkes, 'Krieger und Siedler in Britannien während des 4. und 5. Jahrhunderts', Bericht der Römisch-Germanischen Kommission, 43-44, 1962-3, 155-231.
Hawkes 1972	Note in A. C. C. Brodribb et al., Excavations at Shakenoak III (Oxford 1972), 69-70.
Henshall 1955-6	A. S. Henshall, 'A long cist cemetery at Parkburn Sand Pit, Lasswade, Midlothian', Proceedings of the Society of Antiquaries of Scotland, LXXXIX, 1955-6, 252-283.
Inventorium Sepulchrale	B. Faussett, Inventorium Sepulchrale, ed. C. R. Smith (London 1756).
Jessup 1950	R. Jessup, Anglo-Saxon Jewellery (London 1950).
John 1960	E. John, Land Tenure in Early England (Leicester 1960).
Kent 1967	J. P. C. Kent, 'Problems of chronology in the seventh century in Merovingian coinage', Cunobelin, V, 1967 24-30.
Kirby 1965	D. P. Kirby, 'Problems of early West Saxon history', English Historical Review, LXXX, 1965, 10-29.

Kirk and Leeds 1952-3	J. R. Kirk and E. T. Leeds, 'Three early Saxon graves from Dorchester, Oxon.', Oxoniensia, XVII–XVIII, 1952-3, 63–76.
L'Art Merovingien	Catalogue des Musées Royaux d'Art et d'Histoire Bruxelles, L'Art Merovingien (Bruxelles 1954).
Leeds 1916-17	E. T. Leeds, 'An Anglo-Saxon cemetery at Wheatley, Oxfordshire', Proceedings of the Society of Antiquaries of London, 2nd series, XXIX, 1916-17, 48–64.
Leeds 1936	E. T. Leeds, Early Anglo-Saxon Art and Archaeology (Oxford 1936).
Manning and Leeds 1921	P. Manning and E. T. Leeds, 'An archaeological survey of Oxfordshire', Archaeologia, LXXI, 1921, 227–265.
Manning MSS	P. Manning, Collected Manuscripts, Ashmolean Museum Archives.
Meaney 1964	A. Meaney, Gazetteer of Anglo-Saxon Burial Sites (London 1964).
Meaney and Hawkes	A. Meaney and S. C. Hawkes, Two Anglo-Saxon Cemeteries at Winnall, Winchester, Hampshire, Medieval Archaeology Monograph Series, IV (London 1970).
Mortimer 1905	J. R. Mortimer, Forty Years' Researches in British and Saxon Burial Mounds of East Yorkshire (London 1905).
Müller-Wille 1968-9	M. Müller-Wille, 'Bestattung im Boot', Offa, 25-26, 1968-9, 7–203.
Musty 1969	J. Musty, 'The excavation of two barrows, one of Saxon date, at Ford, Laverstock, Near Salisbury, Wiltshire', Antiquaries Journal, XLIX, 1969, 98–117.
Myres 1954	J. N. L. Myres, 'The Anglo-Saxon Period', in The Oxford Region, ed. A. F. Martin and R. W. Steel, (Oxford 1954), 96–102.
" 1964	J. N. L. Myres, 'Wansdyke and the origin of Wessex', in Essays in British History, Presented to Sir Keith Feiling, ed. H. R. Trevor-Roper (London 1964), 1–27.
Ørsnes-Christensen 1955	M. Ørsnes-Christensen, 'Kyndby', Acta Archaeologica, XXVI, 1955, 69–162.
Peck 1960	C. W. Peck, English Copper, Tin and Bronze Coins in the British Museum 1558-1598 (London 1960).
Peterborough New Town	Royal Commission on Historical Monuments, Peterborough New Town (London 1969).
Rademacher 1936	F. Rademacher, 'Der Trierer Egbertschrein', Trierer Zeitschrift, XI, 1936, 144–166.

Rupp 1937   H. Rupp, Die Herkunft der Zelleneinlage (Bonn 1937).

Skelton 1823   J. Skelton, Engraved Illustrations of the Principal
                           Antiquities of Oxfordshire, ed. F. Mackenzie (Oxford
                           1823).

Smith 1956   A. H. Smith, English Place-Name Elements I, English
                           Place-Name Society XXV (Cambridge 1956).

Speake 1970   G. Speake, 'A seventh-century coin-pendant from
                           Bacton, Norfolk, and its ornament', Medieval Arch-
                           aeology, XIV, 1970, 1-16.

Stenton 1924   F. M. Stenton, 'Personal names in place-names', in
                           English Place-Name Society I, i (Cambridge 1924).

   "   1937   F. M. Stenton, 'St. Frideswide and her times', Oxon-
                           iensia, I, 1937, 103-112.

Steuer 1968   H. Steuer, 'Zur Bewaffnung und Sozialstruktur der
                           Merowingerzeit', Nachrichten aus Niedersachsens
                           Urgeschichte, 37, 1968, 18-87.

Strzygowski 1904   J. Strzygowski, Koptische Kunst (Vienna 1904).

Sutherland 1948   C. H. V. Sutherland, Anglo-Saxon Gold Coinage in the
                           Light of the Crondall Hoard (London 1948).

Van Friezen Franken   Van Friezen Franken en Saksen 350-750, Catalogue
en Saksen 350-750   of the Fries Museum Leeuwarden and the Haags
                           Gemeentemuseum (Leeuwarden 1959 and The Hague
                           1960).

V. C. H. Berks, Bucks,   Victoria County History of Berkshire I (London 1906),
Essex and Oxon   Buckinghamshire I (London 1905), Essex I (London
                           1903), Oxfordshire I (London 1936), V (London 1957),
                           VII (London 1962).

Waddy and Lorimer   C. Waddy and H. L. Lorimer, 'A Scandinavian
              1934   cremation-ceremony', Antiquity, VIII, 1934, 58-62.

Werner 1953   J. Werner, Das Alamannische Gräberfeld von Bülach
                           (Basel 1953).

   "   1954   J. Werner, 'Waage und Geld in der Merowingerzeit',
                           Sitzungsberichte Bayerischen Akademie der Wissen-
                           schaften, I, 1954, 1-40.

   "   1954-7   J. Werner, 'Zwei gegossene koptische bronze-
                           flaschen aus Salona', in Antidoron Michael Abramić I,
                           Vjesnik za arheologija i historiju dalmatinsku, 56-59,
                           1954-7, 115-128.

   "   1961   J. Werner, 'Fernhandel und Naturalwirtschaft im
                           östliche Merowingerreich', Bericht der Römisch-
                           Germanischen Kommission, 42, 1961, 307-346.

White 1969-70

R. White, 'Excavations at Arfryn, Bodedern', Transactions of the Anglesey Antiquarian and Field Club, 1969-70, 257-8.

Wulff 1909

O. Wulff, Altchristliche und mittelalterliche byzantische und italienische Bildwerke I (Berlin 1909).

REFERENCES

1. Bruce-Mitford 1964.

2. V. C. H. Bucks I, 199-204.

3. Proceedings of the Society of Antiquaries of London, 2nd series, XV, 1894, 250-5.

4. Ellis Davidson and Webster 1967.

5. Following Kent 1967, I take 625-630 A. D. to be the date of the ship-burial.

6. Bruce-Mitford 1948, 230-4; Mrs. S. C. Hawkes has suggested that Taplow also was a royal burial, Crowfoot and Hawkes 1967, 65-6.

7. I use the modern word "princely" since it conveys the idea of a man of both considerable wealth and of ruling status, but I do not intend it to imply any precise definition of status and function normally associated with present-day, or even medieval, usage of the word. To have used an Anglo-Saxon word would have required far more space than is here available to justify the choice on the basis of an examination of linguistic and historical evidence for the ranks of Saxon society.

8. Broomfield is, of course, within the kingdom of Essex, and Coombe within Kent, but there is no circumstantial evidence to link them with their respective royal families. In Kent, the burial of royalty within churches began at the start of the seventh century, so that the lack of specifically royal pagan burials in that century is explicable. Were they to exist one might expect them to rival the Sutton Hoo ship-burial.

9. Cole 1959, especially Pls. III-VII, which publish the surviving plans of the old (1679) palace.

10. Proceedings of the Society of Antiquaries of London, 1st series, II, 1852, 280.

11. Akerman 1855, 11, 25, Pls. VI, XIII.

12. e.g. de Baye 1893, 106, Pl. XIV, 4; Baldwin Brown 1915, 467, 485, Pl. CXIV, 3; V. C. H. Oxon I, 352-3, Pl. XXVIII, g, h; also works referred to below, notes 36, 37, 49 and 53.

13. Leeds 1916-17, 49.

14. Ashmolean Museum Archives, letters dated 1936 and 1941 to the relatives and descendants of Bishops Wilberforce, Mackarness and Stubbs.

15. Ashmolean Museum 6" record sheet; Ordnance Survey 25" plan (1939 edition), based on the copy of the 1847 report in Manning MSS.

16. Cole 1959, 61, Pl. IIIc.

17. 1845-6 Estimates and plans for building works and diversion of roads and footpaths, Bodleian MSS, Oxford Diocesan Papers c. 2114.

18. *ibid*. , "new gates" are entered in the Estimate of the expence of founding a demesne round the Episcopal Residence at Cuddesden.

19. Akerman 1855, 11.

20. Church Commission plan dated 1884.

21. Meaney and Hawkes 1970, 39, where besides Winnall II, graves 5 and 10, the following are noted: Burwell grave 83, Melbourn graves 9 and 22, Stanton Harcourt grave 2 and Horndean grave S 18. The discussion is slightly elaborated in Hawkes 1972.

22. Inventorium Sepulchrale, 75, 79; B. Faussett's MS Diary III, 49v, fig. 2, 50, 54; the lace-tag from grave 211 is in the Mayer Collection, Liverpool Museum.

23. Archaeologia, L, 1887, 396; British Museum, Department of Medieval and Later Antiquities Accession Register 1883, 4-1, 228. The grave-group is illustrated in Alcock 1971, Pl. 20.

24. Åberg 1926, 39–40.

25. Information from the excavator, Mr. P. D. C. Brown; I have examined the tags in the Corinium Museum, Cirencester.

26. Peck 1960, 65-6.

27. Akerman's description (Akerman 1855, 11) might seem to corroborate this, for he stated that the skeletons were "accompanied by several objects, among which were" the recorded items (my underlining). But it is clear from his comments on the bucket that he had received no new information on the circumstances of the find, and his description was probably based on his own reading of the 1847 report, rather than on unpublished first-hand information. By mentioning only those objects published in 1847, he implies that had there been other items, knowledge of them was totally lost. Thus it may have been merely his own caution which made him use the phrase "among which".

28. Ellis Davidson and Webster 1967, 1.

29. *ibid*. , 40, contra Evison 1967, 90, where Miss Evison suggested that the finds represented two secondary cremation burials in a prehistoric barrow. The cremated bones were in the bowl, which with all the other grave-goods, was in one grave, 6 ft. below a circle of clay. There would be no hesitation in assuming that the grave was the burial of one man, but for preconceptions about the burial of two swords.

30. Arwidsson 1942, 44–49; Ørsnes-Christensen 1955, 137-8.

31. Arne and Stolpe 1927, 11, 48.

32. Steuer 1968, 60ff., especially statistical tables on 75-87.

33. Inventorium Sepulchrale, 7, 21.

34. Bruce-Mitford 1972, 39 and fig. 3.

35. Inventorium Sepulchrale, 111.

36. Harden 1956, 141-2, 164.

37. Bruce-Mitford 1964, 39-43.

38. Müller-Wille 1968-69, 45-6.

39. Bruce-Mitford 1952, 16.

40. Proceedings of the Society of Antiquaries of London, 2nd series, XV, 1894, 250-5; V. C. H. Essex I, 320-6, Pl. facing 322.

41. Bruce-Mitford 1972, 36.

42. cf. Åberg 1926, figs. 220-221; both the Taplow and Wickhambreux buckles are from very rich graves with Coptic bronze vessels, and the latter also included a blue glass claw beaker.

43. Bruce-Mitford 1964, 21-23, 35-37, fig. 7b, Pl. VIIa.

44. Archaeological Journal, VII, 1850, 36-44; Akerman 1855, Pl. XV.

45. Meaney 1964, 108, gives a full list of references to Aylesford.

46. Jessup 1950, Pl. XXVI, 2; Leeds 1936, 118-120.

47. e.g. Chartham Downs (Kent), Douglas 1793, Pl. V, 1, 7.

48. Harden 1956, 142, n. 38.

49. Proceedings of the Society of Antiquaries of London, 2nd series, XXX, 1917-18, 79.

50. Strzygowski 1904, 264, Pl. XXVIII.

51. Emery 1938, 299, Pl. 75E.

52. Wulff 1909, 214, Pl. LIV, Berlin Museum no. 1022.

53. Werner 1954-7, and revised in Werner 1961, 310-15 and Appendix II, 332-3.

54. de Palol Salellas 1950, 40.

55. Bruce-Mitford 1970, Pl. VIa, b.

56. Bruce-Mitford 1972, 26 and Pl. 5b.

57. Musty 1969, 106, 114-116, figs. 5, 6.

58. Dalton 1912, xxix-xxxiii, xlvii-xlix; there are no exact parallels to the Cuddesdon ring in this work.

59. V. C. H. Bucks I, 204; The Antiquary, XXXVI, 1900, 97.

60. Harden and Treweeks 1945.

61. Excavated in 1954 by Dr. H. W. Catling, who has kindly lent me his excavation records, which I shall be publishing in Oxoniensia XXXVIII for 1973.

62. Wiltshire Archaeological Magazine, XLI, 1922, 312; Meaney 1964, 265.

63. <u>V. C. H. Essex</u> I, 327-8.

64. <u>Proceedings of the Dorset Natural History and Archaeological Society</u>, LXXVII, 1965, 112-3.

65. <u>Peterborough New Town</u>, 4.

66. Fleury 1877, 130-1.

67. <u>Journal of the Royal Society of Antiquaries of Ireland</u>, 2nd series, I, 1856-7, 315-8; the site was re-excavated in 1966 and 1968 by Miss Ann Hamlin, who has generously given me information about this and other sites.

68. White 1969-70; Mr. Richard White is reviewing radial burials from the "Celtic" regions in his forthcoming excavation report in <u>Archaeologia Cambrensis</u>, and has kindly informed me of some of his conclusions.

69. Mortimer 1905, 276.

70. In comparison with prehistoric barrows, Anglo-Saxon ones are notably slight; Asthall and Taplow barrows are somewhat exceptional.

71. For references to Coombe Bissett, Meaney 1964, 274.

72. Bruce-Mitford 1972, 40-41.

73.　　"　　　"　1964, 8.

74. Ellis Davidson and Webster 1967, 9-13, where there is a discussion of the custom and references to other examples.

75. Ellis Davidson 1962, 11-12.

76. At Finglesham several skeletons were entirely removed by grave-robbers, though objects at the head and foot of the grave (commonly vessels) were often left; Mr. A. C. Hogarth kindly allows me to say that similar features have been noted at St. Peter's, Broadstairs, (Kent). This would easily explain why the principal objects found at Cuddesdon were vessels.

77. If the lace-tag is medieval, then both it and the ring might have been lost accidentally on the site: the vicarage and manor house, which were nearby, were both occupied in the fifteenth and sixteenth centuries. One is tempted to ask whether the people who lost these items were the putative grave-robbers !

78. <u>e.g</u>. Uffington, White Horse Hill (Berks), <u>Wiltshire Archaeological Magazine</u>, XLIII, 1926, 437, <u>V.C.H.Berks</u> I, 247; Five Knolls, Dunstable (Beds), <u>Archaeological Journal</u> LXXXVIII, 1931, 193-217; Roche Court Down, Winterslow (Wilts), <u>Wiltshire Archaeological Magazine</u>, XLV, 1932, 568-82; Oliver's Battery (Hants), <u>Proceedings of the Hampshire Field Club</u>, XII, 1932, 9-10; Meon Hill (Hants), <u>ibid</u>., 1933, 127-162, especially 127-139.

79. Procopius, <u>History of the Gothic War</u>, VI, xxv, 7-10.

80. Chaney 1970, 38-41.

81. Waddy and Lorimer 1934.

82. Ellis 1943, 50-58.

83. Letters of Boniface, <u>Monumenta Germaniae Historica, Epistolae Selectae</u> I, ed. Tangl, no. 73.

84. Ellis Davidson and Webster 1967, 11.

85. Ellis 1943, 54.

86. Chaney 1970, 7-120, where this theme is developed.

87. The possibility that the grave had been robbed or incompletely excavated has already been discussed. The thorough robbing of Sutton Hoo mound 2 produced a similar lack of material; but what was found, the use of a ship for burial and the fact that it was in the Sutton Hoo cemetery, leave no doubt of its "princely" quality.

88. For the Roman town, Frere 1962 and 1966, 93; for the Germanic soldiers, Kirk and Leeds 1952-3 and Hawkes 1962-3, 158-169.

89. In 1972 Mr. T. Rowley and Mr. R. Bradley excavated grubenhäuser in the north and south-east of the town (<u>Council for British Archaeology, Group 9 Newsletter</u>, 3, 1972, 15), which complement the one found by Professor Frere in 1962 in the south of the town (Frere 1962, 123-4); material from Bishop's Court House has been discovered at various times since the nineteenth century (<u>V. C. H. Oxon</u> I, 351; <u>Berks Bucks and Oxon Archaeological Journal</u> IV, 1898, 78); the pair of large saucer brooches in Reading Museum, datable to <u>c</u>. 600, may also have come from this site (<u>Archaeologia</u> XXXVIII, 1860, 328, 334); seven inhumations were excavated in 1958 further west of Bishop's Court, one of which contained a narrow seax and seax-shaped knife, datable to the seventh century (<u>Oxoniensia</u>, XXIII, 1958, 131). Mr. Martin Biddle (Biddle 1971, 393-6) has recently made some general comments on such towns as Dorchester-on-Thames, which seem to show a continuity of use from late Roman town, through early Saxon occupation, to early Saxon bishopric, and he has speculated on the royal importance of Dorchester prior to the foundation of the see.

90. These coins are discussed fully by Mr. S. E. Rigold in the forthcoming first volume of the Sutton Hoo publication, and I shall merely refer to them briefly here.

91. Skelton 1823, Dorchester Hundred, 10.

92. I have recently identified this coin as no. 275 in the Heberden Coin Room, Ashmolean Museum; it is a 20 siliquae coin, weight 3.68gm. It is very badly worn, and the edge may have been clipped, but there is no positive evidence to suggest that it had been looped or set in a piece of jewellery.

93. Sutherland 1948, 78, where it is listed as no. 18a, though no. 18b seems to be more likely; Mr. Rigold thinks that both coins may have come from Dorchester.

94. There is a tracing of the sketch of the stud in Manning MSS, and Manning printed an extract from the Minute Book in Berks Bucks and Oxon Archaeological Journal, IV, 1898, 15-16; the stud was also referred to in Manning and Leeds 1921, 241, and V. C. H. Oxon I, 351.

95. The sketch was obviously done very rapidly, and the hasty pen-strokes, which are clearly visible, produced some very misshapen cell-shapes (Pl. IVb); in Fig. 3b, some of the cloisonné pattern has been drawn with greater regularity, restoring it to what is almost certainly closer to its original form.

96. e.g. the pair from Coombe Bissett, Evison 1963, 71, fig. 15b.

97. Werner 1953, 57-60, where one reconstruction is offered; the studs could probably have adjusted straps in other ways; ibid., 89, n. 23 for a summary list of pyramidal studs.

98. Bruce-Mitford 1972, Pl. D.

99.   "   "   1949, Pl. XIVd.

100. V. C. H. Essex I, Pl. facing 322.

101. Proceedings of the Society of Antiquaries of Scotland, I, 1851-4, 217. The circumstances of the find are uncertain. It is possible that it belongs to the same site as a long-cist cemetery of probably early Christian date (Archaeologia Scotica, III, 1831, 41: the reference here states "at the farm of Craigie", while the stud was found "on the farm of West Craigie"). This would be an appropriate context, if the stud did belong, as was stated, to a cross or pastoral staff: it certainly had a bronze core (now lost) and was very worn, features suggesting re-use. Although grave-goods are not normally found in long-cist cemeteries (Henshall 1955-6, 268), it is interesting that the only other Anglo-Saxon material from Scotland, some distinctive seventh-century beads, were also found in Dalmeny parish, in an isolated long-cist (Proceedings of the Society of Antiquaries of Scotland, XLIX, 1914-15, 332-8). Dalmeny's position immediately east of the early Northumbrian monastery of Abercorn is worth noting.

102. Van Friezen Franken en Saksen 350-750, Pl. V, no. 15c.

103. Bruce-Mitford 1949, 52-3, points out the stylistic similarities between the Uppsala stud and the Sutton Hoo jewellery.

104. For a list of these items, Speake 1970, 6.

105. Bruce-Mitford 1972, Pl. 32.

106.   "   "   1949, Pl. IIIc.

107. L'Art Merovingien, 80, Pl. 52.

108. Rademacher 1936, Pl. 6.

109. Bruce-Mitford 1949, 37-39.

110. Since I have not seen the Tongres ornament, I do not wish to put too much emphasis on these comments; the photograph of it suggests that it may be a secondary reconstruction from genuine "Sutton Hoo" pieces of jewellery; the large cabochon settings could be part of this secondary work.

111. e.g. only two cells on the pair of S-shaped brooches from Cividale (Fuchs and Werner 1950, Pl. 35, B49, 50); three on the Heidenheim, two on the Marilles and five on the Täbingen composite disc brooches, the last with three mushroom shapes created from semi-circular and T-shaped cells and a border of stepped half-mushrooms (Rupp 1937, Pl. XXII, 7, 8, 11); four on the Wynaldum buckle, which Bruce-Mitford thought had been made by a Dutch craftsman influenced by Sutton Hoo (Bruce-Mitford 1954); these comments also apply to two English pieces, the Forest Gate (Essex) bead (Jessup 1950, Pl. XXXII, 3) and the Faversham pendant (Åberg 1926, 133, fig. 242).

112. Werner 1953, 40.

113. British Museum, Department of Medieval and Later Antiquities Accession Number 1893, 6-1, 189 (Durden Collection); Proceedings of the Society of Antiquaries of London, 2nd series, XIV, 1893, 314.

114. For a fuller discussion of these problems, Myres 1954, 97-100 and 1964, 18-26; Kirby 1965, 21-29.

115. Cam 1932, especially 370-372; Stenton 1937, 103-112; for the Oxford area, Myres 1954, 100-101 and fig. 33; for a detailed treatment of the evidence for the early history of Abingdon, Biddle et al. 1968, 26-36.

116. Birch, no. 547; the date is wrongly given as 880.

117. Cam 1933, 13-25; V. C. H. Oxon VII, 3.

118. Birch, no. 945.

119. Leeds 1916-17.

120. Werner 1954 and 1961, 327-9.

121. V. C. H. Oxon V, 97-98.

122. For a detailed discussion of the early Anglo-Saxon system of granting estates, John 1960, 39-63.

123. EPNS XXIII, 167-8, where the name is derived from Cūðwine; Stenton 1924, 171, n.5, states the case for *Cuðen being more acceptable.

124. Myres 1954, 99 and 1964, 23-4.

125. Cam and Crawford 1935.

126. EPNS XXIII, 126.

127. ibid., 97.

128. EPNS II, 158.

129. Smith 1956, 291-8.

130. This distribution is based on published place-name surveys, none being available for Lincolnshire, Leicestershire, Rutland, Norfolk, Suffolk, Hampshire and Cornwall; the lack of statistics from several areas of early Anglian settlement may be falsifying the picture, but the negative return from the band of counties between them and the area of dense distribution is well-authenticated.

131. Chadwick 1905, 285-7.

132. Laws of Ine, clause 63, where it is stated that a gesith-born man who leaves his estate may take with him his smith. This could mean goldsmith or jeweller, as well as weapon-smith, especially as a goldsmith would have fulfilled the function of treasurer.

133. As set out in Brothwell 1965, 102-3.

134. ibid., 47.

PLATE I

CUDDESDON GLASS BOWLS: bowl 2 above, bowl 1 below (after Akerman 1855, Pl. VI). Sc. about 1/1.

Photo: R. L. Wilkins

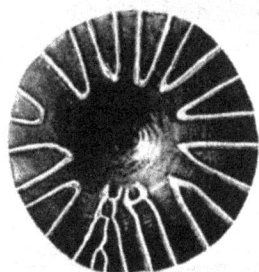

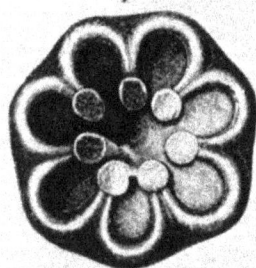

PLATES IIa and IIb

CUDDESDON GLASS BOWL 2. Sc. 1/1

PLATE III

CUDDESDON BRONZE BUCKET (after Akerman 1855, Pl. XIII). Sc. about 1/2.

Photo: R. L. Wilkins

PLATE IVa

CUDDESDON BRONZE FRAGMENT AND MEDIEVAL RING (after Archaeological Journal, IV, 1847, 156). Sc. 2/1 of original engraving.

Photo: R. L. Wilkins

PLATE IVb

DORCHESTER-ON-THAMES PYRAMIDAL STUD (after Society of Antiquaries of London Minute Book XV, 1776, 40). Sc. 2/1.

Photo: T.M.Dickinson

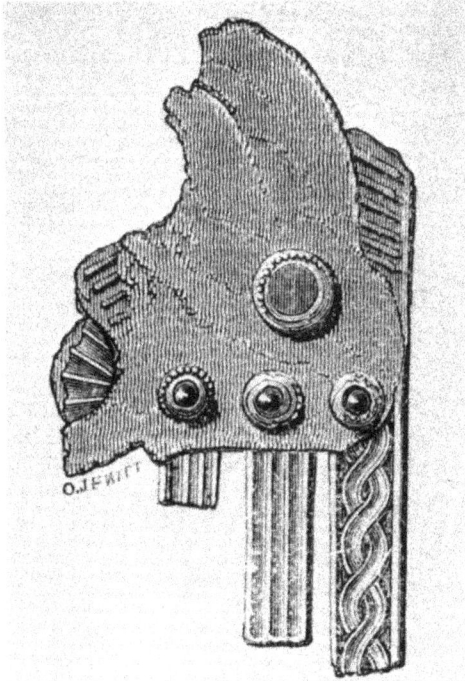

www.ingramcontent.com/pod-product-compliance
Lightning Source LLC
Chambersburg PA
CBHW051309270326
41929CB00029B/3468